How Should I Live My Life?

How Should I Live My Life?

*Psychology, Environmental Science,
and Moral Traditions*

George S. Howard

ROWMAN & LITTLEFIELD PUBLISHERS, INC.
Lanham • Boulder • New York • Oxford

Support for this project was provided by the University of Notre Dame's Erasmus Institute. The time and stimulation provided by the Institute was invaluable and is gratefully acknowledged.

ROWMAN & LITTLEFIELD PUBLISHERS, INC.

Published in the United States of America
by Rowman & Littlefield Publishers, Inc.
A Member of the Rowman & Littlefield Publishing Group
4720 Boston Way, Lanham, Maryland 20706
www.rowmanlittlefield.com

12 Hid's Copse Road
Cumnor Hill, Oxford OX2 9JJ, England

British Library Cataloguing in Publication Information Available

Library of Congress Cataloging-in-Publication Data

Howard, George S.
    How should I live my life? : psychology, environmental science, and
moral traditions / George S. Howard.
        p. cm.
Includes bibliographical references.
    ISBN 0-7425-2206-7 (cloth : alk. paper) — ISBN 0-7425-2207-5 (pbk. :
alk. paper)
    1. Environmental psychology. 2. Conduct of life. I. Title.
    BF353 .H69 2002
    155.9—dc21
                                                                    2002001777

Printed in the United States of America

♾️™ The paper used in this publication meets the minimum requirements of
American National Standard for Information Sciences—Permanence of Paper for
Printed Library Materials, ANSI/NISO Z39.48-1992.

Contents

Foreword

Professor Howard's book *How Should I Live My Life?* encourages us to think long and hard about the future. Specifically, the book demands that we recognize how our present beliefs, desires, political and economic systems, and moral traditions create our future both as individuals and as a society.

Having served in various educational administrative posts for half a century, I have devoted countless hours to the question "How should we educate young men and women to prepare them for the future?" The fruit of my contemplation is a set of five issues that all students ought to confront, in order to give them the intellectual resources they need to be a positive force in the twenty-first century. The issues are (1) peace, (2) justice, (3) an ecumenical view of religion, (4) human rights, and (5) an understanding of the world's emerging environmental problems. This book is important not only because it deals extensively with our emerging environmental problems, but also because it takes a serious look at the role religion has played in the development of our many environmental problems. The book adopts an ecumenical view of religion (considering Christian, Hindu, and Buddhist traditions) and extracts several important insights that promote an earth-friendly philosophy of life.

Humans are the cause of all our emerging environmental problems. Because he is a psychologist, Professor Howard analyzes the human attitudes, habits, and lifestyles that severely stress the earth's ecosystems. Like several others (most notably, former Vice President Al Gore), Howard finds that our environmental problems are more spiritual than psychological in nature. Psychological insights will be most helpful when they lead people to experience spiritual transformations. For example, twentieth-century psychology accepted uncritically the individualism, materialism, and consumerism so prevalent in modern life. But now, psychologists are coming to appreciate the communal, spiritual, and ascetic nature of the environmentally responsible lifestyles that will be required to confront the realities of the twenty-first century. It is most encouraging to hear psychologists searching for answers to eternal spiritual questions, such as "Who are my brothers?" and "Who are my sisters?" and "Am I not my brother's keeper?"

One of the most salient problems in higher education today involves the increasing specialization and isolation occurring within almost all the cognate disciplines. While increased specialization seems to be important for progress to occur in science, a faculty composed solely of ever-more-narrow specialists represents a serious educational problem. If specialists within a discipline experience greater difficulty in communicating their insights with colleagues in different specialties, then what is the prospect for genuine multidisciplinary undertakings? In this book, Howard demonstrates why serious discussions of environmental problems must be multidisciplinary. As you read the book, notice how topics in demography (e.g., global population trends) flow into psychological issues (e.g., the intellectual and psychological effects of family size on children) that have religious implications (e.g., the appropriateness of artificial methods of birth control) and then slide into political and economic considerations (e.g., the aspects of the tax code that favor large families). In analyzing environmental issues one must always keep "the big picture" in mind. While countless disciplines have important insights to make on our environmental problems and their putative solutions, one must be comfortable in the give-and-take atmosphere of multidisciplinary discussions.

Professor Howard's book is now being used with freshmen in a program of four linked courses on the environment. He uses it in a course entitled "Environmental Psychology," which satisfies a university social science requirement. Every student in that class is also enrolled in a biology course entitled "Ecology and the Environment" (satisfying a natural science requirement), a theology course entitled "The Theology of Stewardship," and a philosophy course entitled "Environmental Ethics" (satisfying a theology requirement and a philosophy requirement). It is our hope that considering emerging environmental problems from four independent perspectives will afford students an overview of the interrelated issues, while being exposed to the various intellectual strategies employed by each discipline. This strategy of linking courses on the environment is implemented in the hope that Notre Dame students will come to see knowledge as a tapestry of interwoven strands, rather than a series of largely unrelated forays into separate intellectual disciplines. Finally, the study of environmental problems from multiple perspectives will equip students with the intellectual wherewithal to make positive contributions toward solving some of humanity's most important challenges (along with peace, justice, human rights, and ecumenical views of religion) that cloud our futures.

The emerging environmental problems challenge us to think of large and radical solutions to world problems. For example, it is now clear that the age of using hydrocarbons as our primary energy source is drawing to a close. How will we obtain the energy required to power the hydrogen/electricity economy? Many years ago, I remember discussing an idea for three very large, gossimer-like, thin-film photovoltaic collectors that would float geosyncranously with three great world deserts at an altitude several hundred miles above the earth. The sun would always shine on one or two of these solar energy–collecting space stations. Thus, we would have round-the-clock access to solar power. Getting this energy to the earth's surface posed a problem. Still, I hoped that advances in laser technology would overcome these transport difficulties. Following Stanford Ovshinsky's lead, Howard favors a terrestrial system of solar collectors that immediately store the sun's energy in solid hydrogen storage systems or in huge nickel-metal hydride batteries. Regardless of which system eventually proves most helpful, our young men and women should puzzle through such large, real-world, problem-solution linkages. What better way to learn more about high-energy physics, inorganic chemistry, materials engineering, space travel, developing viable, innovative business models, the economics of scarcity, the clean and renewable technologies of the future, and a host of other related conceptual issues too numerous to mention? The environmental problems challenge us to think clearly, pragmatically, and creatively about some of the most important issues of our time. Isn't that the sort of higher education that all of our children ought to receive?

As you can see, I'm very excited about *How Should I Live My Life? Psychology, Environmental Science, and Moral Traditions*. It is a serious, multidisciplinary analysis of one of the most important issues that we face as a society.

Theodore M. Hesburgh, C.S.C.
President Emeritus, University of Notre Dame

~

PART ONE

Possible Human Natures

One of the ways that language can imprison us is by defining something as singular when the realities to which the words refer clearly are plural. "Human nature" is one such concept. Some would have us believe there is only one, immutable human nature. Thus, the title "Possible Human Natures" leaves some readers a bit uneasy.

Human nature does change (albeit, very slowly) through random genetic mutation coupled with selective retention (i.e., biological evolution). Sadly, this sort of evolution works far too slowly to be of significant help with the environmental problems we now confront. Cultural evolution (Ehrlich 2000; Ornstein and Ehrlich 1989) ranges from change in our beliefs about issues that are relevant to the environment, to the way I (or we) change social institutions (e.g., alternative energy investments, the tax code) to alter our ways of thinking, feeling, and behaving. The ways that words and ideas can produce cultural evolution that lead to more earth-friendly human natures are presented in part I of this book. Part II deals with structural changes in our lives (both as individuals and as societies) that will make it easier for all of us to tread more lightly on this planet. Chapter 1 outlines the project for this book.

Chapter 2 begins by laying my philosophical cards face-up on the table. Our looming environmental crises pose challenges in all intellectual domains. Psychology is as relevant as physics; chemistry as implicated as cultural studies; economics as central as ecology; and our geology as critical as our gods.

Thus, our underlying philosophies (of science, of nature, and of the good life) must be as flexible as the problems and perspectives we seek to explore. Chapter 2 explains how we can be ontological realists when speaking of biological, physical, and chemical realities while adopting more constructivist positions when speaking of our attitudes, cultures, and gods.

In my opinion, human beings are best understood as self-determining, story-telling agents (Howard 1989, 1993). Chapter 3 elaborates on human natures (as we currently find them in the Western world at the dawn of the twenty-first century) from this narrative, agentic perspective. In large part, humans create themselves psychologically via the foundational stories (e.g., liberal democracy, free market capitalism, Christianity) that they tell themselves as if those stories were literally true. Then, chapters 4 and 5 focus upon two of the general themes (i.e., perfectionism and maximization) that are particularly harmful for the worldviews and lives of moderation and voluntary simplicity that are needed for the twenty-first century—if humans are not to overstress our planet's ecosystems.

CHAPTER ONE

~

Introduction: Why Change Is Needed

In his presidential address to the American Psychological Association, Donald Campbell (1975) warned against psychology's tendency (as well as the tendency in American society in the early 1970s) to contradict and denigrate the wisdom offered by traditional, societal institutions such as educational systems and religions. Campbell's talk represented a heroic act, as it flew in the face of the "anything goes" or "let it all hang out" *zeitgeist* of the mid-1970s. The core of Campbell's argument was that traditions and institutions (such as religions and schools) that had withstood the test of time embodied a deep wisdom that had been winnowed over centuries (sometimes millennia) of experience. Psychologists, Campbell argued, were far too willing to overthrow such highly evolved sources of wisdom when these institutions' teachings seemed to be contradicted by psychological research or current fads within our profession.

Campbell was correct. Traditional societal institutions have been subjected to withering criticism over the last fifty years. We need to examine the extent to which the philosophy of life and the philosophy of human nature that we currently believe *as if they were literally true* have changed from the beliefs held (say) fifty years ago. Thus, a part of this book represents social criticism. But I must first quickly demonstrate why social criticism is appropriate. The short answer is that a host of global ecological threats now loom before us. You've all heard of global warming, ozone depletion, deforestation, desertification, vanishing biodiversity, acid rain, soil poisoning, and the like. But these are effects, not causes. So let's take a few minutes to understand the basic *causes* of these varied, troubling ecological effects.

Ecological Trends and Projections

There are many ways to tell scientific tales of the future. Perhaps the least controversial approach is simply to state current scientific theories and to plot the present trends of the variables implicated as important by those theories. Ehrlich and Ehrlich (1991) noted that the stress placed upon any ecosystem by humans can be determined by consulting the following formula, $I = P \times A \times T$. In this formulation, the impact (I) of any group is the product of the size of its population (P), its per capita level of affluence (A) as measured by consumption of goods and services, and a measure of the damage done by the technologies (T) employed in supplying each unit of that consumption. An ecosystem's carrying capacity is defined as the population size that an ecosystem can sustain indefinitely. When the human population's total impact (I) exceeds the ecosystem's sustainable carrying capacity, the ecosystem begins to deteriorate. Unless human impact is reduced, an ecosystem pushed beyond its carrying capacity will deteriorate until it eventually crashes (Wilson 1992).

Counting the number of humans in a population is a reasonably straightforward task and, so, determining the value of P is relatively easy. Figure 1.1 shows the course of P over the past thousand years. Any reasonable person who examines this graph will realize that our species is now experiencing out-of-control growth. The results of this growth might be catastrophic for the health of our planet's ecosystems.

Measuring the population's affluence level (A) is much more difficult because combining entities such as land, water, air, energy, and so forth into one overall measure is problematic. GDP (gross domestic product) has traditionally been used to measure a population's level of affluence (A). The technology (T) term is often mistakenly thought to signify an antitechnology bias in the $I = PAT$ equation. T simply reflects the environmental *destructiveness* of the techniques used to produce the goods and services consumed. In fact, sophisticated technologies can obtain either high or low values assigned for T. For example, complex technologies, such as nuclear-powered electric plants, can have high values for T because society cannot safely deal with radioactive waste for the thousands of years that it requires attention. Similarly, chlorofluorocarbons (CFCs)

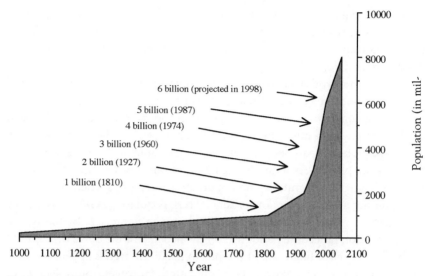

Figure 1.1.   Global Population Growth

used as aerosol propellants, as cleaning detergents for microprocessors, and for heat transfer in cooling units once were considered to be commodities with a low, assigned value of T. But CFCs' value for T first increased when they were found to be greenhouse gases and then increased again when they were implicated in the destruction of the earth's ozone layer, which protects us from the sun's ultraviolet rays. Thus, the value assigned for T is always a function of science's state of knowledge of the entities and techniques in question. In chapter 9 we'll see a very complex technology—photovoltaic cells within roof shingles—that produces electricity and has a value for T of about 0.

Unfortunately, there is currently no accepted procedure for obtaining worldwide values for T. Values can be estimated only on a technology-by-technology basis. However, several scientists (e.g., Ehrlich and Ehrlich 1991; Holdren 1990, 1991) have suggested that a measure of a population's energy consumption serves as the best available index of the combination of affluence and technology (A x T). This is because several disparate entities (e.g., forests lost, oil burned) can be converted into energy unit equivalents with little distortion. Also, the amount of waste produced by human activities is now closely related to the amount of carbon-based energy consumed (Ehrlich and Ehrlich 1991). What energy consumption (as a measure of A x T) hides is the fact that not all sources of energy stress ecosystems equally. For example, obtaining electricity from solar power stresses the earth far less than obtaining electricity by burning coal. What are the current paths of P, A, and energy consumption (A x T) in the above I = PAT formula?

I know of no worldwide figures of the growth in energy consumption and GDP. However, the growth in energy consumption, GDP, and population in developing countries over a 30-year period is shown in figure 1.2. Although a 30-year time span might be large for psychological studies, it represents a deceptively short span for the physical and biological trends that now threaten the planet. As with all restriction of range problems, one tends to underestimate the magnitude and importance of relations when they are assessed during a narrow window of time. Thus, population, GDP, and energy use *appear* to grow in a linear fashion as shown in figure 1.2. Similarly, the standardization procedure performed on the dependent measures (using 1960 as the base year) in figure 1.2 also tends to make the trends appear less dramatic than if the raw data had been presented. However, the trajectory of growth in the global human population can be interpreted as a *geometric* (or exponential) trend (Malthus 1798/1964) when considered over a much longer period of time—such as the second millennia of our common experience (see figure 1.1). In reality, the increases in GDP and energy consumption in figure 1.2 are even steeper (and more troubling) than the growth in population depicted in figure 1.1.

Since the Industrial Revolution, the planet's human population (P) and the amount of energy consumed by humans (A x T) have increased geometrically. This represents an inherently unstable situation that must be corrected. [Kenneth Boulding, former president of the American Economic Association, stated the problem succinctly, "Only madmen and economists believe in *perpetual* exponential growth" (quoted in Hardin 1993, 191).]

What—If Anything—Can Be Done?

Facts do not cease to exist because they are ignored.

—Aldous Huxley

If the future reveals that predictions of impending ecological destruction are correct, who will bear the lion's share of blame for this tragedy—a catastrophe foreseen but not avoided? Human beings will undoubtedly be blamed, since too many humans and their ever-expanding consumptive

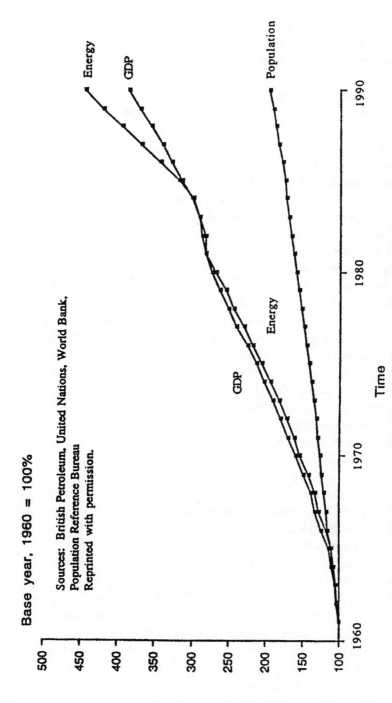

Figure 1.2. Growth in Energy Use, GDP, and Population, Developing Countries, 1960–1991. [From Lenssen, N. (1993). Providing energy in developing countries. In L. R. Brown (ed.) *State of the world*. New York: Norton, 1993. Reprinted with permission.]

activities represent the root causes of all ecological problems. But, more specifically, what about humans will be seen as having produced ecological catastrophe? Two obvious candidates are human nature and human cultures. We've now moved to topics of psychology and social criticism.

Let's consider human nature first. The overriding command of evolution is to become reproductively successful. An obvious strategy for accomplishing this goal might be to reproduce the maximum number of offspring possible. So perhaps the command to overpopulate our planet lies buried in our genes. However, the path of evolution suggests that *lower* organisms tend to employ a "replicate many thousands of times so that a few might survive" strategy. Higher organisms are more likely to reproduce a limited number of times, and then work to enhance the survival rate among their offspring. Thus, it is unlikely that our genes crudely compel humans to reproduce as often as possible. In all likelihood, we receive a more subtle genetic message.

A second piece of evidence, that humans are not hardwired to reproduce to the maximum, comes from the fertility rates of women across time and across cultures. Across time, fertility rates have tended to drop somewhat. However, these declines are dwarfed by the differences found between cultures at any point in time. For example, using 1991 figures, women in Italy average 1.3 children over their childbearing years, whereas women in Tanzania average 7.1 children. Exactly how "genetically preprogrammed" can humans be when women in one culture reproduce more than five times as frequently as women who live only a few thousand miles away? Rather, it seems the huge cultural differences between Italy and Tanzania are responsible for their stunningly different fertility rates.

The same pattern emerges when one examines the second engine of ecological destruction—namely, overconsumption, or unsustainable lifestyles. Undoubtedly there are genetic presses toward increased consumption; however, the variability among consumption rates in current cultures is so enormous that it suggests that cultural differences hold the key to effectively reducing the kind of consumption now stressing the earth's ecosystems. For example, a child born in the United States in 1990 will consume more than sixteen times the energy (and thus produce approximately sixteen times the waste) over his or her lifetime as a child born at the same time in India. This is not to imply that Americans are naturally wasteful while Asian Indians are by nature conservationists. Rather, American children are raised within an extremely wasteful system. Perhaps America's current, wasteful energy system holds clues as to how First World countries might create more earth-friendly lifestyles for themselves. Part II of this book, entitled "Reengineering Wasteful Systems," will outline how inappropriate economic and business systems can be reengineered to allow for human consumption (i.e., maintaining high levels of A [affluence] in the I = PAT formula) without overstressing fragile ecosystems.

Free market capitalism represents the dominant belief system that currently buttresses our lives and businesses. It has been argued that a free market capitalist system will inevitably lead to human overpopulation and overconsumption, and thus this belief system represents an impediment to creating more earth-friendly cultures and lifestyles. This book argues that this is not necessarily the case! In fact, a reformed free market capitalist system is actually capable of *reducing* human overconsumption. However, several distortions to our present free market system must first be rectified.

The values of democracy and free market capitalism come as close to fundamental beliefs for citizens of the First World as any assumptions one might mention. While I prefer democracy to any other political system, and free market capitalism to any other economic system, both approaches (as currently practiced) possess drawbacks that might be explored and modified with profit. Certainly a close examination of politics, as practiced in many democracies today, reveals that there is much room for improvement (consider the current state of partisan politics, PACs, the absence of "political courage," voter apathy, etc.). Still, who among us would rather live under a feudal system, a fascist dictator, a communist state, or any other political arrangement?

An important way that one expresses his or her love for any belief system is to critique its shortcomings when one sees concrete changes that might serve to enhance the belief system as practiced. For example, I have critiqued the Catholic church's opposition to artificial means of birth control (Howard 1993, 1994a) and science's inability to experimentally demonstrate freedom of will in humans (Howard 1994b; Howard and Conway 1986). Science responded well to my suggestions regarding the role of self-determination in the genesis of human action; the Catholic church remains unmoved on the basic morality of artificial methods of birth control. You win some, you lose some. The eventual outcome of our suggestions for improvement is less important than the fact that we try our best to improve the belief systems and institutions that we cherish.

While I would love to improve upon democracy as it is currently practiced, I possess no good ideas for improving our political system, so I will remain silent on this topic. However, my studies in ecological psychology

(Howard 1997) reveal a set of insights that hold enormous potential for improving our current free market capitalist system. First, let's ask a question.

What Is Free Market Capitalism?

George Will, one of capitalism's staunchest supporters, offers the following definition:

> Capitalism is an enveloping culture of restless striving by individuals [who are] broadly emancipated from constraints on seeking the satisfaction of their multiplying appetites. It is a permanent revolution. (Will 1983, B9)

Capitalism seeks to foster a culture of multiplying appetites. People are instructed to want more out of life, to have more this year than last year, and to want a better life for their children than they themselves have. Mr. Will claims that capitalism places its faith in the belief that "restless striving by individuals" serves as the engine for continued progress, so long as this striving is emancipated from constraints. The American version of free market capitalism has (probably wisely) declared its opposition to certain forms of constraint, such as monopolies, price controls, and undue governmental intervention. However, there is another set of constraints that will prove difficult for the future of capitalism, namely, the ecological limits of human activity on the earth. We have returned to I = PAT. The central problem with the Atlantic world's form of free market capitalism is that it worships at the totem of maximum human consumptive activity. It champions the creed that consumption will bring happiness. Thus, Madison Avenue annually produces billions and billions of dollars' worth of propaganda that repeatedly brainwashes us and our children to their (i.e., business) version of "reality." Are you unpopular? Buy a racy, gas-guzzling car. Are you feeling a bit lonely today? Swill some mouthwash and smear on more deodorant. Feeling isolated? Pick up a cell phone, pager, and portable FAX machine. Then—and only then—will you begin to feel better. By the way, please put all of these items on one of your thirty pieces of plastic, so that we can take an additional, usurious 21 percent APR out of your pocket.

I just said my piece pretty crudely—George Albee made similar points in proper, scholarly prose.

> The capitalist system, in order to sell its plethora of manufactured goods, has had to enlist the help of the motivation researcher and the Madison Avenue

ad agency to get rid of the excessive and ever growing pile of manufactured goods not really needed in our society. To encourage consumption in the absence of real need and to associate status and self-esteem with wasteful consumption, it has been necessary to encourage relatively mindless impulse buying and self-gratification. By now, we have raised several generations of people on endless and repetitive exhortations that it is all right to yield to impulse, to buy without guilt, and to consume without shame. Installment buying may have been the fatal blow to the self-denial of the Protestant ethic. (Albee 1977, 150)

Madison Avenue's advertisement propaganda, that people adopt wasteful, consumption-oriented lifestyles, represents an important ecologically destructive force against which children and adults need to be inoculated. Contrary to the consumerist vision of life, wasteful overconsumption, unbridled greed, and short-term myopia must be understood as destructive vices. [Note here that all First World countries are subject to the critiques herein to some degree. I choose to describe the American version of this problem for two reasons. First, I know the American scene far better than I know, for example, the European situation. Second, the American situation is arguably the worst example of individualism and overconsumption, and thus represents the strongest instance of this contemporary malady.]

How do you like the title of this book? Did you say to yourself "That's interesting! I think I'll read it?" In one sense, it's a deeply flawed title—I purposely demonstrated one of our contemporary problematic beliefs in the title. Did you catch it? The title should have read "How should we lead our lives?" Why should we focus upon the *group* rather than the *individual*, you may ask? Well, let me answer by asserting that I believe that the thorny psychological issues of the twenty-first century will be social in nature, not individual. How can I give you a sense for the shift in problem-types that is now taking place?

Try to think of people's behavior in terms of "paying costs" (in the present) and "reaping benefits" (in the future). It takes time for some "costs" to produce certain "benefits." Consider a few behaviors. Exercising? Sinning? What about studying? Drinking too much alcohol? If I drink too much, do all of us get sclerosis of the liver—or only me? If you exercise and I don't, do both of us lose weight and look better? While you can do things to make all these activities and their consequences social, generally speaking they are individual.

Now think of some important ecological behaviors. Having a large family? Consuming carbon-based energy? Recycling? The ecologically important behaviors of the twenty-first century will be different-in-type from the behaviors psychologists dealt with in this past century. Virtually all members of the *group* pay equally for individual "ecological sins" regardless of who commits them. If everyone else chooses to have children, we all live in a horribly overcrowded world even if you sacrifice and only have one or two children. If Saddam Hussein decides to detonate every oil well in Kuwait, all of us live in a more polluted world, not Saddam alone. It seems to me that nearly all of the ecological problems we now face are of this "individual acts right now lead to group consequences later" sort.

Prisoner dilemma games have shown how tempting it is for people to shoot for the maximum possible payoff—to tempt others into cooperating while the individual competes. In economics, this leads to the prevalent and devastating problem of the "free rider." The ultimate consumerist dream is for the individual to be able to consume without conscience or consequence— but this can only safely occur if most other group members live spartan, virtuous lives. We have generalized our consumptive profligacy to "generation abuse" through our tendency to live fat and rich for today and lay off the consequences upon our children and their children. This seems to be true whether the consequences are depleted stocks of nonrenewable natural resources (e.g., polluted air, soil, and water) or obscene levels of national debt. (Do you know how many tax dollars are required *each day* to pay the interest on the U. S. national debt?)

In fact, over the course of my lifetime the vice of gluttony has been raised to the highest of all human characteristics. Many social scientists go so far as to actually assume that gluttony is the most fundamental of all human tendencies. But the word "gluttony" has too negative a valence to be cleaned up and made respectable. So we smuggled the concept into polite conversation under the term "maximization." Herrnstein (1990) correctly noted that belief in the maximization/optimization vision of human action now represents social scientists' most basic, unexamined assumption about human nature— expressing its poison through theories of reinforcement maximization, utility maximization, maximizing the number of genes one passes into the next generation's gene pool, and the like. Table 1.1 presents a few "killer (or faulty) thoughts" from our wasteful twentieth century. In part I of this book we thoroughly examine the role of some holdover beliefs from the twentieth century (e.g., maximization, consumerism, perfectionism) that will prove toxic in the twenty-first century. In the third section of this book we consider human beliefs, taken from moral traditions, that will promote a sustainable society for the twenty-first century.

Table 1.1. Killer (Faulty)Thoughts: For a World with Limits

1. Consumption will produce happiness (and consumption is "needed")
   - I'll be happy when I get that new Lexus, my home on the beach, etc.
   - Shopping as a form of relaxation; catalog shopping; The Shopping Network
   - The belief that if consumers stop buying, then people will lose jobs
2. The future is to be steeply "discounted"
   - We are the "Now generation," so we don't need to think (or worry) about the future
   - We'll "worry about that later"
   - Buy now—make no payments until next year (as individuals given a line of credit, or as a nation with an enormous national debt)
3. Present consumption is preferred to investment in (or conservation for) the future
   - Short-term rewards and punishments are greatly overvalued relative to long-term consequences in the calculus of decision making
   - No one speaks for the rights of the next generation (i.e., draining the Social Security trust funds)
   - Debt is now as natural as breathing
4. Growth is good
   - GDP must always increase
   - An undeveloped resource is a wasted resource
   - More of a "good" (e.g., people, products) is preferred to less
5. Free market capitalism is the best system
   - "Greed is good"—we should all get as much as we can
   - The CC-PP game (communized costs—privatized profits) (Hardin 1993)
   - Systems should encourage greater human economic activity (throughput)
6. Paying less (for something) is better than paying more
   - Cheap gas (or electricity, or water, etc.) is preferred to expensive commodities regardless of their real, total costs
   - Keep prices as low as possible by externalizing whatever costs possible
   - Government support for "commons situations" (e.g., leasing federal land for grazing) is a great "deal"
7. If it ain't broke (yet), don't fix it
   - Collapse occurs long after an ecosystem's carrying capacity has been exceeded
   - We don't need to act for the sake of "uncertain" projections about, for example, global warming, ozone depletion, food shortages, etc.
   - If it's not my problem, it's not a problem (e.g., Social Security, starvation)
8. Until scientists can prove a phenomenon beyond scientific doubt, society doesn't need to act on it
   - No one can prove that smoking causes lung cancer
   - Risks should be managed by the free market
   - Ecological threats are more like people (innocent until proven guilty) than like drugs (guilty until proven innocent)
9. Innovations (technological and others) can push back biological limits indefinitely
   - Malthus was "wrong" because of the "green revolution"
   - We don't need to worry about unintended, negative consequences of technological "solutions" (i.e., solutions often produce a new and different set of problems). The "next" technological breakthrough will solve the problem
   - Some still think we could ship excess people to another planet

Source: (Howard 1997, 55–56).

Who'll Stand Against the Idols of Our Age?

I now need to make a transition to the wisdom contained in those ancient institutions and traditions that Campbell praised so highly in his presidential address to the APA in 1975. If we now believe that the meaning of life lies in maximizing rewards, experiences, consumable pleasures, your bank account, and so forth, then what ancient wisdoms about human nature (and the good life) have been forced out by our contemporary worldviews by our newer, warmed-over views of gluttony?

Thirty years ago every educated person knew what story was alluded to by the phrase "the golden mean." Do we now know it? Similarly, every kid in my high school knew what "moderatio in omnia" meant—not now.

Table 1.2. Teachings of World Religions and Major Cultures on Consumption

Religion or Culture	Teaching and Source
American Indian	Miserable as we seem in thy eyes, we consider ourselves . . . much happier than thou, in this that we are very content with the little that we have. (Micmac chief)
Buddhist	Whoever in this world overcomes his selfish cravings, his sorrows fall away from him, like drops of water from a lotus flower. (*Dhammapada*, 336)
Christian	It is easier for a camel to go through the eye of a needle than for a rich man to enter into the kingdom of God. (Mark 10:25)
Confucian	Excess and deficiency are equally at fault. (Confucius, XI.15)
Ancient Greek	Nothing in Excess. (Inscribed at Oracle of Delphi)
Hindu	That person who lives completely free from desires, without longing . . . attains peace. (Bhagavad-Gita, II.71)
Islamic	Poverty is my pride. (Muhammad)
Jewish	Give me neither poverty nor riches. (Proverbs 30:8)
Taoist	He who knows he has enough is rich. (Tao Te Ching)

Sources: Compiled by Worldwatch Institute, Durning (1992).

Finally, I wonder how many of us know where the phrase "the middle way" originated? I'll give you a hint—it quickens the heartbeat of almost half the people on the face of the earth. But how many Americans know its origin? Try on the subversive, antimaximization sentiments found in table 1.2.

Collectively they hint at the role that moral traditions might play as a counterweight to a cultural milieu that valorizes consumerism, maximization, materialism, and other gentrified forms of gluttony.

Maximization is one example of a larger sickness that stalks social life to-day—the disease is extremism. It spawns a brood of petty vices that slowly rob us of character, nobility, and class. The brood includes perfectionism, the belief that winning is everything, the notion that "to the victor go the spoils," fundamentalism, demonizing one's opponents, litmus tests of ortho-doxy, partisan politics, the belief that "might makes right," and a host of other bigoted, ungenerous beliefs and attitudes. While I'm no fan of George Bush (the elder), I think he had it right when he hoped for "a kinder and gentler world." Our beliefs now make our world a colder, crueler place with each passing year.

What conclusions might we draw from this diverse sample of observa-tions? First, I believe that the ecological crises that we are now beginning to experience will be the leading causes of human pain and suffering in the twenty-first century. Thus, psychologists like myself must become involved with the crises' etiology, prevention, and treatment. Second, these crises rep-resent symptoms of maladies that lie at the very heart of our contemporary worldviews and societies. Third, the cures of these maladies lie in human be-liefs (and human lives) that are governed by character and virtue. However, character and virtue are tendencies that are in short supply these days. I agree with Donald Campell's claim that the modern undermining of institutions that champion the development of virtue in young lives (i.e., religions, edu-cational systems, sports, the Boy and Girl Scouts, etc.) has left the door open for various selfish, mean-spirited worldviews such as consumerism and maxi-mization notions of various sorts.

So, what's my solution? I'll bet some of you think I'm calling for a return to "that old time religion" or some massive governmental program to spend our way out of this huge ecological mess. You couldn't be more wrong. I rec-ommend governmental action to help us to behave more virtuously in our public lives. Here my model is not Al Gore's (1992) "global, ecological Mar-shall plan," but rather George Will's (1983) "statecraft as soulcraft." The specifics of this model need to be fleshed out in this book.

CHAPTER TWO

~

Constructive Realism

Many have suggested that a paradigm shift is occurring in the philosophy of the social sciences. The previous paradigm that has dominated the modernist era during the twentieth century could be characterized as objectivism or realism. The new paradigm, which could be described as a constructivist perspective, is based on the assumption that personal realities are socially constructed. This perspective assumes that there can be no observations that are independent of the observer.

As you know, in the Constructivism-Realism debate we generally identify ourselves as favoring one or the other pole of this dichotomy. Our intellectual opponents, of course, are fanatically committed to the most extreme interpretation of the opposite pole. So this chapter's title "Constructive Realism" might be seen as a ploy on my part to seize the middle ground—which is the position that will enrage the maximum number of combatants. If I only succeed in being controversial in this chapter, I'll consider my effort a failure. I'd like to think that more is going on than all of us blowing hot air at one another as we pass the time between now and our deaths.

Perhaps when one tries to put opposites together, one will only get incoherence—rather than helpful integration. *Constructive realism* might represent nothing more than a highfalutin oxymoron. I don't think that is the case, but honesty demands that I might be too much of a moron to understand some deep incoherence in my putative solution. Thus, unless I do some serious, insightful work soon, you'll surely vote thumbs down on this chapter. Academics generally get serious by first defining their concepts. How to define constructivism and realism? Well, I'm tenured, so it doesn't really matter if readers think I'm a little less than "properly scholarly." Consequently, I'll offer definitions that are, for me, enormously insightful and fruitful, but they don't look like proper scholarly definitions. With profound thanks to Efran, Lukens, and Lukens (1988), I offer the following atypical definition of constructivism and realism that, oddly enough, puts an emphasis on different *types of people* rather than on scholarly turf.

> Objectivists are inventors who think they are discoverers—they do not recognize their own inventions when they come across them. Good constructivists, on the other hand, acknowledge the active role they play in creating a view of the world and interpreting observations in terms of it. (28)

Constructivists are discoverers who think they are inventors—they tend to downplay the role that "real worlds" [either *out there* or (for psychologists) *in here*] play in our experimental (and clinical) observations. Good realists, on the other hand, always strive to appreciate the nature of the objective realities that had a hand in creating the useful, but imperfect, observations that we experimentally (and clinically) construct.

Do you know what I like about that definition? It allows me to say that I'm a little bit of both—some days I feel more like an explorer, other days I could swear I'm a creator. Similarly, and *most* importantly, on some topics I could swear I'm creating things, while on other topics I'm virtually certain I'm mostly reading the real world out there. Would you like an example of that last point? What are you—a realist or a constructivist—on the topic of cold fusion and on the topic of God? I know those are not typical topics for psychologists, but please bear with me, as I am working toward a solution to the constructivist-realist problem that, I hope, applies across the entire landscape of the sciences and the humanities. A solution that says something like the following: "physicists are almost always better off thinking of themselves as realists; theologians on the other hand are better off being constructivists." And what of psychologists? I think we are perched midway between the humanities and the hard sciences—which is why we ought to see ourselves as *constructive realists* and not as extremists on either pole. Unfortunately, it is more difficult to handle the intellectual ambiguity contained in an integrated metaphysics (e.g., constructive realism) than it is to be myopicly committed to either extreme position. But I'm afraid that I ran all that by you quite quickly. Let's back up a step and first consider the problems of God and cold fusion a bit more carefully.

A Modest Ode to Realism

In a recent article in the *International Journal of Psychology and Religion* I was talking about (what else?) cold fusion. As usual, I was making eminently reasonable, totally noncontroversial claims. Because I was discussing a topic in physics, I was leaning toward an objectivist construal of the issue of cold fusion. In discussing the role of reason in science, I said,

> The recent Pons and Fleischmann controversy over "cold fusion" is a good example of a radical concept that the scientific community entertained but (for now) has chosen to reject due to insufficient compelling theoretical articulation and experimental evidence. Although advocates of cold fusion might feel their ideas have received overly harsh critique by an inappropriately conservative organization, the majority of scientists today believe these innovators were treated fairly—as the background theorizing and experimental evidence are not now sufficiently compelling to warrant altering long-held theories of physics. Finally, it is possible that with a handful of years of additional experimental and theoretical development a number of current physical theories might themselves change in response to the challenge of cold fusion. So although scientists are open to new ideas, they take a very conservative attitude toward them. (Howard 1993)

A constructivist reactor (who also happened to be overly enamored by the Edinburg strong program in the Sociology of Knowledge) took exception to the objectivist construal that I gave to the cold fusion debacle. Since he believed all "facts" are nothing more than social constructions, he found my suggestion—that characteristics of the physical world might be responsible for cold fusion's failure—rather unpalatable. He offered a different view of cold fusion's failure.

> In fact, the cold fusion controversy had amazing little to do with evidence or theory. It had more to do with such issues as the fact that Pons and Fleischmann were chemists, not physicists, that they announced their findings by press conference and not journal publication, and the fact that their research threatened multimillion dollar high-energy physics grants of those who were working on "hot fusion." In fact, the statements of these two scientists were nearly drowned out by the harrumphing of "regular" scientists dismissing them out of hand. (Donahue 1994)

Although all the "heat" that the constructivist notes did in fact occur, it was not the *cause* of the scientific community's rejection of cold fusion claims. The reactor's "reasons" serve to explain why professional heat accompanied the rejection, not *why* the scientific claims themselves were rejected. This constructivist sees the effects of bad science (and also bad professional demeanor by Pons and Fleischmann), and he wrongly assumes these reactions were the *cause* of the rejection by the scientific community. Donahue is wrong in this claim—pure and simple. If virtually unlimited amounts of heat could be produced by passing a weak electric current through a bucket of cold water with salt, only a thorough paranoid would believe that a politically constructed collusion by a powerful scientific elite could cover up such a startling discovery. Don't you think that the University of Utah would now be pursuing cold fusion with complete abandon to cash in on the billions of dollars that would flow from its patents, if only they could make the process work? The journal *Philosophy of Science* summarized the lessons to be learned from the cold fusion controversy in the following way.

> In retrospect, it is difficult to draw any conclusions other than that Pons and Fleischmann were careless in their work and announced stunning results based on little and flawed evidence. This was compounded by their refusal to admit their errors and to withdraw their (by then) baseless claims. The most obvious "heavy" in the entire episode is James Brophy, the vice president for research at the University of Utah, who pressed for early announcement by the chemists and who remained active at the center of the financial and legal intrigues that followed. *But what has this to do with the methodology of science?* Not much. What is relevant, though, is the way the scientific community studied the claims and eventually rejected them, in spite of an initial commitment on the part of many investigators to corroborate the claims of Pons and Fleischmann. This is important if one wants to view science as a social phenomenon shaped by societal forces. For, while it is true that science collectively had a vested interest in the "received" views on nuclear fusion that it had established over the previous fifty years or so, it is also the case that there were great pressures, from industry, financial institutions and the public in general, to substantiate the Pons and Fleischmann claims. But, it just could not be made to fly. While it is undoubtedly so that evidence does not uniquely determine a theory, it is as true that not just anything can be made to go in science. (Cushing 1994, 2)

So what do I want to conclude from this digression into cold fusion? Clearly, the world of physical realities out there represents a most important element in determining *which* scientific theories will pass muster and which won't. If we see physics as nothing more than a socially constructed collusion by a scientific power elite where any old theory can be made to go—then I think we miss a crucial element in why physics works as well as it does.

An Equally Modest Ode to Constructivism

Now let's jump to the opposite extreme. Are you a realist or a constructivist on the problem of God? Well, speaking for myself, I was raised with an oppressively objectivist view of religion. As Sister Stella Regis always said, "There is but One True God, and His only begotten son, Jesus, became man so that we could become faithful members of the One, True, Holy, catholic (small c) and apostolic Catholic (big C) church and if any of you lousy kids don't believe that 100 percent then when you die you're gonna be *toast!*" As you can see, Sister Stella wasn't a fan of nonobjectivist construals of God— and she also wasn't overly enamored with understatement. But Sister Stella's intellectual tastes aside, we must recognize that there are currently billions of people alive who have a completely objectivist construal of God—*they know* God and all of God's characteristics, beliefs, and wishes for us—and they know them right down to the cores of their beings. The obvious intellectual difficulty with this situation is that there have probably been at least a thousand different religions. Thus, in order for any subgroup of several millions of these theists to be correct in their objectivist construal of God—then several billion of the rest must be wrong in their construal. My reading of the evidence on the existence and characteristics of God is that most of the array of God-stories are about equally compelling—and, unfortunately, God has remained conspicuously silent in helping us to pick out the one, true God from the welter of false Gods and religions. So whether or not God created humans—I believe history has shown that *humans construct their Gods*. While I am largely an objectivist on questions of atomic fission, hot and/or cold fusion, and the like, I am a constructivist on the question of God.

In philosophy of science I learned one distinction that is quite important indeed. That is the distinction between epistemology and ontology. Epistemology has to do with how we come to know things, and ontology deals with the nature of things in themselves—things like atoms, centers of gravity, brains, selves, rumors, and gods. When I pledged allegiance to realism on the issue of cold fusion and to constructivism on the problem of god, did I mean ontologically, epistemologically, or both? Recall that at the start of this chapter I claimed that a constructivist perspective "is based on the assumption that personal realities are socially constructed.

This perspective assumes that there can be no observations that are independent of the observer." So obviously I see us as epistemological constructivists. What I've been examining above is whether we're also to be ontological constructivists. I feel that psychologists take grave risks if they do not realize that there are real forces that form human action—genes, endorphins, neural circuits, physical environments, cultures, kinship systems, and many more. Thus, we ought to be at least partially (and perhaps largely) ontological realists. Extreme ontological constructivism seems to me to be just plain silly. I'll stay near the golden mean on this issue. That is, while we are moved by the socially constructed beliefs of others, we're also impacted by genes, endorphins, and so forth.

And while I just suggested that all of us might want to think of ourselves as epistemological constructivists, let's take another, closer look at that possibility. While I think that there are no observations that are *independent* of the observer, does that imply that *all* observations are created equal? Are we to completely give up the Holy Grail of objectivity?

I'm endorsing a position like Donald Campbell's famous "We are to be ontological realists and epistemological fallabilists." But being a fallabilist is *not* the same as believing that there is no reality out there, or that there are not more objective measures possible of that reality. Far from arguing that any old observation was as good as any other—or that any social construction might be as helpful as any other—Campbell himself did the pioneering work on the preeminent technology for actually improving fallible, scientific observations. [Here I refer to construct validity as approximated through the multitrait-multimethod matrix analyzed via structural equation modeling.] I fear I've already made too much ado about metaphysics, so I'll leave it for now.

Constructive Realism and Looming Environmental Crises

Rather than plowing forward on philosophical issues, I'll instead turn to a general critique of current intellectual styles, and then finish with my hope for the type of constructive realist psychological scholarship that might carry us into a better twenty-first century.

There is a strong tendency in humans to think in dichotomous, either/or terms (Rychlak1989). The difficulty with dichotomous thinking is that in asserting the importance of one pole of the dichotomy, one might implicitly downplay the importance of its presumed polar opposite. The history of scholarship in psychology repeatedly demonstrates that thinking in terms of either/or dichotomies can prove unhelpful. For example, is heredity or environment more important to development? Should one adopt masculine or feminine characteristics? Are you a believer in free will or determinism? In these, and many other issues, we find some value in the perspectives represented by both polar opposites. For example, would the free will–determinism antinomy have persisted for over 2,000 years, if there was absolutely no value in either of the presumed antagonistic perspectives? Happily, psychological scholarship repeatedly moves past unhelpful dichotomies, toward more nuanced appreciations of the ways that oppositional perspectives enrich one another. In such instances, either/or frames might be replaced by both/and conceptualizations. Thus, we now understand the roles of both heredity *and* environment in human development (Plomin 1990), free will *and* determinism in the genesis of human action (Howard 1994b), masculinity *and* femininity in sex-role orientation (Constantinople 1973), perspective of rights *and* perspective of care in moral development, both innocent *and* guilty in issues of legal culpability (Howard 1992), and so forth. Adopting "both/and integrations" where society tempts us to see issues in terms of "either/or dichotomies" will make us less likely to fall into the traps of radicalism, fundamentalism, extremism, and maximization that stalk contemporary intellectual life.

Think of this as a general guideline for making intellectual commitments. You ask me if I'm an ontological constructivist or an objectivist? I hope you now better realize how I can say that I am both—more of one than the other if the topic is physics, the opposite if we speak of religion, and generally equal parts of constructivist and objectivist when the topic is psychology. Am I anti-abortion or pro-choice? You guessed it, I'm both. Am I a free willist or a determinist? You've got the pattern by now, I'm both a free willist and a determinist—because that ancient controversy wouldn't have endured for over 2,000 years if there weren't important truths in both perspectives. Similarly, I am both a realist/objectivist *and* a constructivist because both perspectives contain important insights.

I believe it was Carl Hempel who first exclaimed, "What is the world that the mind can know it? What is the mind that it can know the world?" Let's start with the first part, "What is the world that it can be known by mind?" Well, there are some theories about the world—like cold fusion—to which the world will simply not acquiesce. Similarly, while the world will not let humans fly, no matter how fast they flap their arms, birds are allowed to fly by flapping their wings. And it's not that the world rejects all attempts by humans to fly because it is opposed to humans flying—the world's laws are neutral in the sense that the workings of aerodynamics are the same for birds as for humans.

In summary, our scientific explanations must not be incompatible with certain aspects of our objects of investigation, or the theory simply will not fly because the world won't let it. However, the world will *not* veto all theories but the One, True Theory of (for example) human nature. Philosophy of science would be a whole lot easier if the world acted only that way. The Truth would then be contained in the one theory (and the only one) that passes scientific muster. What could be easier? We know nothing until we find the Truth. But—alas—the world and science just don't act that way.

Why anyone would assert that one's currently favored scientific theory tells him or her anything about the (Capital T) Truth about the world is a mystery to me. Such people simply don't understand that science doesn't tell us anything about Truths. Rather currently favored scientific theories are those that are in closest accord with the epistemic criteria for theory choice—such as predictive accuracy, internal consistency, external coherence, unifying power, fertility, and so forth—no more, no less. Thus the phrase "scientific Truth" is oxymoronic. Why anyone would worry that a "scientific Truth" contradicted a "religious Truth" [an equally oxymoronic phrase] is beyond me.

Let's now address the question, "What is the mind that it can know the world?"

Assume for a moment that there is a real world "out there" (or "in here" for psychologists) that might be known scientifically. What are the chances that *our minds* might come to know it perfectly? Or know it objectively? Or know it at all?

First, let me assert that Donald Campbell was absolutely correct when he observed wryly, "Cousin to the amoeba, how could we know perfectly?" So—even assuming a knowable world—please forget the dream of a perfect scientific knowledge. Similarly, the extreme relativists' fantasy that "anything goes"—that everyone's opinion on a topic is as valid as anyone else's opinion—is just plain wrong also. This can easily be demonstrated in physics, demonstrated (with difficulty) in psychology, and reasonably argued in religion.

Let me summarize the beliefs that follow from my ruminations thus far:

1. There are some realities out there (and in here) that must be given their due if we want to construct scientifically compelling stories.
2. Being cousins to the amoeba, we cannot know anything perfectly. Thus all knowledge is flawed. Consequently, all talk about (Capital T) Truths serves to get us into trouble—whether we speak as scientists or as members of a faith tradition.

3. For me, the key is to be a committed empiricist (à la William James's principle of radical empiricism) in my search for understanding. Were I a physicist, I'd be a researcher who was looking for nature's laws in the traditional way—although always on the alert for the philosophical curve ball (such as Einstein's relativity, Heisenberg's uncertainty, Bohr's interpretation of complementarity) that our scientific excursions might turn up. As a psychologist, I am broadly empiricist (using quantitative and qualitative methods, and even, on occasion, developing a few new research approaches to fill holes in our current cadre of methods). I also try to adopt as many conceptual perspectives as possible (e.g., free willist, phenomenologist, narrativist, biological reductionist, radical behaviorist, social learning theorist) in order to appreciate both the somewhat fixed and the somewhat malleable (i.e., constructed) aspects of what it is like to be a human being.

4. I'm even a committed empiricist in my role as a nonprofessional theologian. I am not a believer in Jim Jones's religion (Jonestown) or David Koresh's faith (Waco) because the fruits of these belief systems do not reflect well on these religions (in my opinion).

But there is yet another way in which I'm a committed empiricist in religion. Imagine that at this time next week I find myself riding on an ass from Jerusalem to Damascus in order to torture and murder some godless, radical constructivists if they are unwilling to convert to the one, true faith of Constructive Realism. Suddenly, the skies darken and I say "Whoa assey! This don't look so good." A bolt of lightning then knocks me off the donkey and I think, "No big deal! People get struck by lightning all the time—I'm just glad to be alive to interpret the experience." But when a booming voice says, "George, George, why doest thou persecute righteous constructivists so?" *That's* when it becomes a non-natural experience for me. The voice orders, "You are no longer to be called George, henceforth you are to be known as 'Stupid.'"

"I've always thought stupidity was an underappreciated characteristic," I reply. "I'm thrilled to be known as 'old stupid.' By the way, Lord, how do your friends address you?" If the voice says, "Yahweh," I'm suddenly Jewish. If God says, "Allah," then I believe in Islam. If "Buddha," I'm Buddhist. If "Jesus," I'm Christian. If the voice says, "Zoroaster," I'm momentarily confused. But so great is my commitment to empiricism that eventually I'd be thrilled to be known as "Stupid the Zoroastrian!" Unfortunately, all of the experiences of my life thus far seem to have reasonable, natural (as opposed to supernatural) explanations, so my choice of a religious belief system is of necessity based upon more pragmatic considerations. However, I'd love to experience a slightly less dramatic [than my version of the Saul-becoming-Paul story] critical experiment in the religion domain but I haven't—yet. One more point, and then I'll be finished.

What is the import of the constructivism-realism debate for environmental issues? First, we must be ontological realists in our analyses of all looming environmental problems. To paraphrase, realities will not change if we ignore them. Also, we cannot place faith in modern-day versions of the *deus ex machina* sleight of hand. Cop-outs like "there is no limit to human ingenuity, so someone will find a solution," or "all of these problems will be solved by the action of free markets," and so forth, are intellectually bankrupt efforts to stop discussions of important (but psychologically troubling) issues. It is disingenuous to argue that human ingenuity and free markets worked to create environmental problems (and then the miracle occurs) so that now they will solve the problems they just created. The ostrich strategy has always been recognized as impotent by everyone—except the ostrich!

The coming environmental crises—the effects of overcrowding, global warming, loss of biodiversity, overstressed waste sinks, etc.—represent real physical/biological problems that must be dealt with in real, efficacious ways. These problems will not simply be wished-away.

While the past is set in stone, the future is still open to human intervention. The beauty of the constructivist perspective is that it can help us to realize that we are creating our futures day-by-day. We can explore several possible futures and then choose which one we (both as individuals and as a society) will work to try to create.

In conclusion, this chapter might be seen as an ode to the "golden mean." More and more I've come to distrust extremism, perfectionism, absolutism, and radicalism in almost any form. In fact, I've even adopted a motto of sorts. "Extremism—even in the service of a good cause—is to be deplored by reasonable people." With respect to this realism-constructivism issue, I'd recommend that we all resist the urge to endorse either extreme view—and think seriously about becoming Constructive Realists.

CHAPTER THREE

~

Stories, Stories Everywhere;
But Not a Truth to Think

Prelude: That Reminds Me of a Story . . .

In *Quiz Show* (Redford 1994), Professor Charles Van Doren Jr. is a Columbia University professor who wins instant fame (the cover of *Time* magazine) and fortune (more than tenfold his academic salary) for winning for fourteen straight weeks on the television quiz show "Twenty-one." Young Charlie is a popular teacher, he is finishing an important book on Abraham Lincoln, and weighing a fabulous job offer to be the educational consultant for NBC television. So why, with all this success, is young Charlie so agitated and unable to sleep?

Charles Van Doren Sr. (also a Columbia classicist) can only see Charles Jr. as a chip-off-the-old-block, "Don't worry, Charlie. I always went a little nuts as I was ending a book. Why, your mother almost left me as I was finishing my book on Carl Sanberg." But the audience knows that something else lies behind Charlie's angst. He hasn't earned his victories on the quiz show—the show's producers supplied the answers in advance. But what's the problem? Charlie's rich and famous; "Twenty-one's" audience ratings have gone through the roof; and the show's sponsor's sales have increased by over 50 percent. Isn't that the way entertainment and capitalism are supposed to work? Where's the problem in all this success?

Charlie's moral crisis crystallizes when a reporter (who is aware that he is interviewing a celebrity who is also an expert on Lincoln) asks, "Professor

Van Doren, how do you think Honest Abe would have done as a contestant on Twenty-One?" While easily able to dodge the reporter's question, a tormenting examination of Charlie's conscience has begun that eventually leads to a public confession of his misbehavior that jeopardizes both his financial and academic futures. Charlie knowingly chooses to be more like Honest Abe rather than emulate the rich and famous captains of industry with whom he has now become involved.

Would Charlie have had his conversion experience if the reporter had asked, "Professor Van Doren, how do you think the Great Emancipator would have done as a contestant on Twenty-One?" That question also identifies Lincoln, but it refers to a different *story* about the man—an equally important story—but one that is irrelevant to Charlie's crisis. Charlie has not been a racist, he's been dishonest. It also might have been unhelpful to refer to Lincoln as the Hero of the Civil War, Defender of the Union, or the Country Lawyer from Illinois, for these designations also conjure up stories of Lincoln that would be irrelevant to Charlie's particular dilemma. Of course, Honest Abe didn't have a monopoly on the virtue of honesty. Does the statement "Father, I cannot tell a lie. I chopped down the cherry tree" ring a bell for you? Or, have you ever seen a parent glare at a child and ask, "Did I just see your nose grow a little longer?" Less-than-truthful children know to quickly review the object lesson of the story of their favorite little wooden boy. Honest Abe means nothing to most kids—Pinocchio probably would have been brushed-off by Professor Van Doren. How is it that real and fictional stories can create moral orders and individual virtues that then serve to steer human's actions through the rocky shoals of life?

The Scottish clinician Miller Mair made a remarkable claim when he observed that

> Stories are habitations. We live in and through stories. They conjure worlds. We do not know the world other than as story world. Stories inform life. They hold us together and keep us apart. We inhabit the great stories of our culture. We live through stories. We are *lived* by the stories of our race and place. It is this enveloping and constituting function of stories that is especially important to sense more fully. We are, each of us, locations where the stories of our place and time become partially tellable. (Mair 1988, 127)

Polkinghorne (1988) makes a similar point, "We make our existence into a whole by understanding it as an expression of a single and developing story"

(150). And McAdams (1985) notes the role of story-telling in the development of identity.

> My central proposition is that identity is a life story which individuals begin constructing, consciously or unconsciously, in late adolescence. As such, identities may be understood in terms directly relevant to stories. Like stories, identities may assume a good form—a narrative coherence and consistency—or they may be ill-formed. . . . The life story-model of identity suggests how the personologist, or anyone else seeking to understand the whole person, may apprehend identity in narrative terms. Furthermore, the model suggests hypotheses about identity which can be tested in research, and less rigorously, in personal experience. (McAdams 1985, 57–58)

According to such theorists, the essence of human thought can be found in the stories we employ to inform and indoctrinate ourselves as to the nature of reality. But how do we human beings grow into our role as *homo fabulans* (i.e., man the story-teller)?

While human infants might not have the sort of hardwired instincts often seen in many infrahuman species, children certainly do have some strong tendencies or predispositions. The two related tendencies that I wish to focus upon are language use and the use of stories in the struggle toward finding meaning in one's experiences.

Let us now consider some central aspects of a narrative approach to psychology. These aspects are better illustrated if we consider a case study that David Leavitt described in his novel *The Lost Language of Cranes* (1986). He uses a story as an interlude between chapters. This story is a kind of key to the book—one that deals with homosexuality and coming out of the closet. Based on a true account of a clinical case, it tells us about *The Crane-child.*

> A baby, a boy, called Michel in the article, was born to a disoriented, possibly retarded teenager, the child of a rape. Until he was about two years old, he lived with his mother in a tenement next to a construction site. Everyday she stumbled in and around and out of the apartment, lost in her own madness. She was hardly aware of the child, barely knew how to feed or care for him. The neighbors were alarmed at how Michel screamed, but when they went to knock at the door to ask her to quiet him, often she wasn't there. She would go out at all hours, leaving the child alone, unguarded. Then one day, quite suddenly, the crying stopped. The child did not scream, and he did not scream the next night either. For days there was hardly a sound. Police and social workers were called. They found the child lying on his cot by the window. He was alive and remarkably well, considering how severely he appeared to have

been neglected. Quietly he played on his squalid cot, stopping every few seconds to look out the window. His play was unlike any they had ever seen. Looking out the window, he would raise his arms, then jerk them to a halt; stand up on his scrawny legs, then fall; bend and rise. He made strange noises, a kind of screeching in his throat. What was he doing? The social workers wondered. What kind of play could this be?

Then they looked out the window, where some cranes were in operation, lifting girders and beams, stretching out wrecker balls on their single arms. The child was watching the crane nearest the window. As it lifted, he lifted; as it bent, he bent; as its gears screeched, its motor whirred, the child screeched between his teeth, whirred with his tongue.

They took him away. He screamed hysterically and could not be quieted, so desolate was he to be divided from his beloved crane. Years later, Michel was an adolescent, living in a special institution for the mentally handicapped. He moved like a crane, made the noises of a crane, and although the doctors showed him many pictures and toys, he only responded to the pictures of cranes, only played with the toy cranes. Only cranes made him happy. He came to be known as the "Crane-child." (Leavitt 1986, 182–83)

The true stories of Charles Van Doren Jr. and the "Crane-child" serve as bookmarks to highlight the way that stories can create character and the possession of certain (and not other) virtues in each of us. The role played for Van Doren by the "Honest Abe" story is quite understandable to the type of people who would read this chapter. Which of the Jesus stories has been most instrumental in forming your character as a Christian? Mine is the one about the good shepherd who had a hundred sheep, but one of them wandered away. . . .

While you might have difficulty "believing" or "understanding" the Crane-child story, most clinical psychologists see it as a believable (though extreme) example of common occurrences they see in their practices—people who tell themselves unusual stories about the nature of reality. [Having co-authored a book (Bartholomew and Howard 1998) that analyzed over two hundred documented cases of claims of "alien abduction," the Crane-child doesn't look terribly extreme to me!]

The moral to be extracted from this excursion into how the stories we "choose" to tell ourselves (as if they were literally true) serve to create our character might best be summarized by a gloss of a remark by Hamlet, "Beware of the stories you tell yourself, for you will surely be lived by them."

Finally, the more radical claim that all thinking is some form of storytelling (which is elaborated upon later in this chapter) was anticipated by Gregory Bateson,

A man wanted to know about mind, not in nature, but in his private large computer. He asked it (no doubt in his best Fortran), "Do you compute that you will ever think like a human being?" The machine then set to work to analyze its own computational habits. Finally, the machine printed its answer on a piece of paper, as such machines do. The man ran to get the answer and found, neatly typed, the words: THAT REMINDS ME OF A STORY. (Bateson 1979, 2)

Culture Tales

One typically begins a fairy tale with the phrase "Once upon a time. . . ." This introduction serves to tip-off the reader as to the genre of the story being offered. Thus, when the author speaks of fairies, dragons, leprechauns, and the like, the listener is not unduly troubled—for imaginary creatures routinely roam the world of fantasy. Lots of strange, fanciful possibilities can be comfortably entertained in a fictitious story. However, there are other story-forms where talk of fictitious creatures is forbidden. For example, even at Notre Dame, one could not get away with a research proposal that purported to study the role of incentives in learning by leprechauns.

The acute ear should be troubled because I just made an important claim in the context of the quip about research on leprechauns. I implied that science was another form of story-telling; and thus of the same genus as fairy tales, although undoubtedly of a very different species. But that is precisely the claim being made herein. If it can be shown that science represents a case of meaning-construction via story-telling, then the more general hypothesis that most forms of thought reflect instances of story elaboration becomes quite plausible. Finally, by demonstrating the storied nature of all thought, I believe that my ultimate goal—namely, proposing that cultural differences might be rooted in the preferred stories habitually entertained by ethnic, class, racial and cultural groups—might gain a degree of credibility.

Does the Notion of "Story-Telling" Degrade Human Thought?

Have we demeaned human thought by suggesting that it is nothing but story-telling? To answer, consider what might be a competing explanation of human mentation. One of the oldest views of mental processes (dating back at least to the very beginnings of Western civilization) is that humans are rational and logical beings. Are humans rational and logical? Indeed sometimes they are. However, psychological research continually turns up ways in which humans are imperfectly logical (e.g., Nisbett and Ross 1980) or logical thinkers with limited capacities (e.g., Simon and Newell 1964). But one might wonder: Are humans innately rational and logical? While that question might never be answered definitively, any student of human thinking knows that there are numerous instances of irrationality in human thought and action. That rationality and irrationality persist, despite our culture's diligent efforts to teach rational modes of thinking, suggests that rational thought represents a singular achievement for individuals, even if we might be naturally disposed to think rationally.

Narrative psychologists (e.g., Bruner 1986; Howard 1989; Mair 1989; McAdams,1985, 1993; Polkinghorne 1988; Sarbin 1986; Spence 1982) would want to make a slightly different claim. Logic or rationality represents *a type* of story (or kind of analysis) that one might choose to apply to a particular problem (or situation) in order to understand the issues at stake, and discover plans of action that one might entertain. So, through education and practical experience, we might learn to solve problems logically and rationally. But obviously there are many instances where one is instructed to entertain storylines other than logic and rationality. [Seeing aspects of one's life through the eyes of religious belief is but one, obvious example.] So the narrative psychologist believes that scientific theories represent refined stories (or rich metaphors) meant to depict complex causal processes in the world. And when human thought turns to issues of "what caused something to occur," many would argue compellingly that scientific stories represent the best analysis available. However, when our thinking is drawn to a consideration of issues of meaning in our lives (e.g., What do I wish to achieve in my life?; What would be the moral or ethical action in a particular circumstance?; What is the good life?), scientific stories might lack the rich resources of other nonscientific perspectives like philosophy, literature, clinical wisdom, religion, and the like. The moral is: different types of stories best serve different functions. Some important scholars now take quite radical positions on this point. For example, Kenneth Gergen claims, "It is my view at this point that the separation between fact and fiction is only one *of style*, and that the scientific style is the inferior in many ways because of the enormous number of limitations by which it is encumbered. (How many experiments do you know, about which anybody cares?)" (Gergen 1989, personal communication).

One should realize that even mathematical thinking is story-telling. Mathematical stories involve the workings of abstract symbol systems where the demand for internal consistency (that there be no logical inconsistencies within the system) is paramount. This reality was brought home to me a few years ago as my children watched a "Smurfs" cartoon where the Smurfs were trying to free a captured princess by solving the following riddle:

$$4X + 3Y = 23$$
$$2X - 2Y = 8$$

I took a piece of paper and began solving the simultaneous equations, in the hope that my 3- and 4-year-old boys would (1) be impressed with their dad's knowledge of riddles and (2) recognize that the benefits of education sometimes pop up in the strangest places (like Smurf cartoons). I first took the second equation and solved it for X—as I had learned in high school—to yield:

$$X = Y + 4$$

By then substituting Y + 4 for X in the first equation, or so the story goes, one will obtain a value for Y:

$$4(Y + 4) + 3Y = 23$$
$$4Y + 16 + 3Y = 23$$
$$7Y = 7; Y = 1$$

Now replacing 1 for Y in either equation will yield a value for X. Replacing Y with 1 in the first equation yields

$$4X + 3 = 23$$
$$X = 5$$

One is able to check the accuracy of these results by substituting the obtained values of X and Y (namely, 5 and 1 respectively) into the second equation, and noting whether or not it is a balanced equation:

$$2(5) - 2(1) = 8$$

Thus, our solution is correct. Armed with the key that would unlock the Smurf princess from her unjust imprisonment, I awaited the perfect moment to dazzle my sons with my bit of mathematical magic. A statistician friend was staying as our house guest at that time. He walked into the room just as I finished my calculations, and asked what I was doing. When I showed him the equations and explained that the safety of the princess hung upon the Smurfs accurately solving this algebraic riddle, my friend paused for about 15 seconds, and then stated matter-of-factly "X = 5, Y = 1." While my friend is smart, there is no way he could have solved the problem that quickly by using my method. He must have known a different story (or method, or algorithm) for solving simultaneous equations, so I asked how he did it. He traced the outline of an approximation technique whereby he guessed at initial values of X and Y and revised those guesses in light of the direction in which his computed values missed the original equations' values (namely, 23 and 8). I had never before been told that story for solving simultaneous equations with multiple unknowns. But that story works also. By the way, the Smurfs rescued the princess—without needing to solve the algebraic riddle. My kids still think math is boring and their dad is a nerd.

This "mathematics is a process of following story lines" position can be demonstrated in the most simple cases also. Consider the following problem:

Problem	Step 1	Step 2	Step 3
23	23	23	23
x 46	x 46	x 46	x 46
	138	138	138
		92	92
			1058

The multiplication sign (x) tells us we are not telling an addition story, nor a subtraction tale, nor a division fable. Multiplication stories proceed in the following manner: first multiply the top number by the right hand part of the bottom number, and put that result under the line (Step 1); then multiply the top number by the left hand part of the bottom number and put this value under the first value (but you must move this second value one place to the left of the first value under the line) (Step 2).

Why do you move this second product one place to the left? I haven't a clue—that's just the way the multiplication story goes. But you have to tell this multiplication story in exactly this manner in order for it to work (i.e., to yield the correct answer). Put the second product directly under the first (or two places over to the left) and you get the wrong answer every time. The climax to the multiplication story comes when you add these two intermediate products (Step 3).

Follow the story line perfectly, and you'll *usually* get the right answers (unfortunately, computation errors do sometimes occur). Are there other ways of multiplying? Yes there are. The abacus, for example, tells a different tale of how to achieve the correct outcome.

Why have I spent this much time suggesting that mathematics can be seen as learning how to tell mathematical stories? Similarly, why did I (Howard 1985, 1991) argue that scientific theorizing involves telling stories that maximize the values inherent in the epistemic criteria (i.e., predictive accuracy, internal consistency, external coherence, fertility, and unifying power) for theory choice? If we can reasonably understand scientific and mathematical reasoning as instances of story-telling, it should not be difficult to imagine other forms of human thinking (e.g., practical reasoning, intuition, pathological thinking) as instances of story-telling also. This is not to demean human thinking—it simply sees several forms of thinking as important variations on a central theme, namely, story-telling. And so, might not our cultural differences be due, at least in part, to the differing stories that we learn as part of our socialization into different cultures? And further, might the stories we are telling ourselves as if they are literally true (e.g., the nine "Killer Thoughts" presented in chapter 1) actually be the *causes* of our overly wasteful lifestyles that are, in turn, causing the degradation of so many of our planetary ecosystems?

Culture: Some of the Stories We Live By

LeVine (1984) defines culture as "a shared organization of ideas that includes the intellectual, moral, and aesthetic standards prevalent in a community and the meanings of communicative actions." (67). He further emphasizes that a recurrent experience of ethnographic anthropologists "is that they [anthropologists] are dealing with shared, (supraindividual) phenomena, that culture represents a consensus on a wide variety of meanings among members of an interacting community approximating that of the consensus on language among members of a speech-community" (LeVine 1984, 68). Thus, a culture can be thought of as a community who "see" their world in a particular manner—who share particular interpretations as central to the meaning of their lives and actions. From this perspective, education can be understood as the initiation of the young into the dominant meaning-systems of that culture. In a more negative construal, one might see indoctrination rather than initiation. Translated into the terms of this book, the young learn to believe and tell the dominant stories of their cultural group—be those stories scientific, civic, moral, mathematical, religious, historical, racial, economic, or political in nature. As individuals tell increasingly more deviant stories (and act upon those antisocial beliefs) they are labeled as criminals (if the deviant story and subsequent actions have an antisocial theme), or mentally disturbed (if the story is not so much illegal as it is different from accepted notions of "reality"). Thus, institutionalization of criminal deviants can be seen as (1) protecting society from further infection by illegal beliefs and acts, (2) punishing individuals to reduce the likelihood they will act illegally in the future, or (3) concentrating the criminal element so that members can become even more conversant with the criminal point of view and more closely enmeshed within the criminal subculture—as many critics of our judicial and penal systems fear. A similar analysis could easily be offered for the practice of institutionalizing psychologically disturbed members of our society.

Then what kinds of stories does our culture suggest we entertain as fundamental? As already noted, rational, logical, mathematical, and scientific story lines are highly regarded. But the preponderance of Americans also report strong religious beliefs, belief in our democratic political institutions, belief in the importance of the family, and a plethora of other value commitments. So one might assert that we are urged to entertain a pluralistic stance toward thinking about life. Depending upon the nature of the issue, the circumstances involved, and one's objectives at the time, any of a number of disparate story lines might be called upon to make sense of a particular issue. Being able to consider issues from a number of different perspectives (a skill demonstrating cognitive flexibility) is generally praised as the mark of an educated, perceptive citizen. While we might in our professional roles (e.g., scientist, politician, religious leader, mathematician) specialize in particular types of story lines (e.g., scientific, political, religious, mathematical), one mark of a liberally educated individual is his or her ability to consider problems or issues from all the perspectives deemed legitimate by our American culture. But, of course, some types of stories (e.g., astrology, witchcraft, sorcery) are deemed illegitimate at this time in our culture, and thus are generally not taken seriously.

Modern anthropology thoroughly demonstrates the collective and organized nature of each culture. One does not need large numbers of informants to learn the dominant stories of any culture. Virtually all competent adult members of a culture can repeat the consensus view on a variety of storied meanings in their culture. And unlike earlier anthropological findings, modern ethnography consistently finds cultures to evidence organized, coherent belief systems.

No ethnographer who has followed Malinowski's (now standard) program for intensive fieldwork has failed to find increasing connectedness and coherence in customs—particularly in their ideational dimension—as he or she becomes better acquainted with their meanings in vernacular discourse and practice. There is controversy about the degree and kind of coherence—claims that cultures are deductive systems, pervasive configurations, seamless webs, have been repeatedly made and just as often disputed—but even those most skeptical of cultural coherence would not return to the earlier view of customs as discrete traits. The "shreds and patches" concept of culture has simply not survived the test of intensive field investigation, because the ethnographer, in learning to communicate with people of another culture, discovers the orderliness not only in their communicative conventions but in their version of "common sense," the framework of ideas from which they view, and act upon, the world. The framework may not be as orderly as a syllogism or a formal taxonomy, but it is far from a random assemblage of discrete elements. Most important, it is an organized set of contexts from which customary beliefs and practices derive their meaning. (LeVine 1984, 72)

Of course, the history of anthropology amply demonstrates that the dominant stories of other cultures have not always been accorded legitimacy by Western cultures. Cultures organized around the wisdom of a set of stories that are quite different from our (i.e., Western) dominant cultural tales were labeled as "backward" or "primitive" cultures—even by anthropologists. Shweder (1984) shows a long history of what he calls "Enlightenment thought" (e.g., Frazer 1890; Turiel 1979; Tyler 1871) in anthropological thinking. Enlightenment thought, "holds that the mind of man (sic) is intendedly rational and scientific, that the dictates of reason are equally binding for all regardless of time, place, culture, race, personal desire, or individual endowment, and that in reason can be found a universally applicable standard for judging validity and worth" (Shweder 1984, 27). To an anthropologist of an Enlightenment temper, Western culture was the paradigmatic example of a rational, scientific belief system. Therefore, any culture's distance from this Western ideal became the measure of its backwardness or primitiveness. Other cultures weren't merely different from ours—they were seen as inferior to our culture. This Enlightenment myopia not only gave certain Western anthropologists grounds for their brand of cultural elitism, but it also served as a set of lenses through which they could view their professional tasks and goals.

From that Enlightenment view flows a desire to discover universals: the idea of natural law, the concept of deep structure, the notion of progress or development, and the image of the history of ideas as a struggle between reason and unreason, science and superstition. (Shweder 1984, 28)

But there has always been a countertheme to this Enlightenment approach in anthropology. The Romanticist view (e.g., Geertz 1973; Levy-Bruhl 1910; Whorf 1956) holds "that ideas and practices have their foundation in neither logic nor empirical science, that ideas and practices fall beyond the scope of deductive and inductive reason, that ideas and practices are neither rational nor irrational but rather *nonrational*" (Shweder 1984, 28). The Romanticist view is implicit in "symbolic" anthropology (e.g., Geertz 1973; Sahlins 1976; Schneider 1968; Turner 1967) wherein nonrational ideas (presuppositions, cultural definitions, declarations, arbitrary classifications) are of paramount concern. Or as Shweder (1984) says it, "Indeed the main idea of a symbolic anthropology is that much of our action 'says something' about what we stand for, and stands for our nonrational constructions of reality" (45). Nonrational constructions of reality are what one gets from stories. Stories slice the world up (or urge us to view the world) from a variety of different perspectives, points of view, and value positions, and thus construct noncomparable frames of reference through which reality might be grasped. One can view reality from a political perspective, as an ethical exercise, scientifically and empirically, rationally and logically, superstitiously, aesthetically, or from any of a number of other frames of reference.

> The whole thrust of Romantic thinking is to defend the coequality of different "frames" of understanding. The concept of nonrationality, the idea of the "arbitrary" frees some portion of man's mind from the universal dictates of logic and science, permitting diversity while leaving man free to choose among irreconcilable presuppositions, schemes of classification, and ideas of worth. (Shweder 1984, 48)

Returning to the theme of "thinking as instances of story-telling" that was developed at the beginning of this chapter, we can see that anthropologists in the Romanticist tradition have no trouble seeing different stories as embodying differing themes, perspectives, or frames of reference. Further, the Romanticist would want to argue for the fundamental noncomparability of different perspectives, such as racial tales, religious narratives, political themes, scientific perspectives, family narratives, and so forth. Different frames present differing views of reality. But no one frame is superior to another. The anthropologist in the Enlightenment tradition, on the other hand, argues that scientific and rational visions of culture and history are not only *different*, but also *better* perspectives from which to view cultural differences. So while all anthropologists might see the stories a culture habitually invokes in understanding its reality as being important in the formation of its unique cultural identity, there would be great disagreement as to whether all stories are created equal. Science and rationality would be the obvious candidates for deification by Enlightenment anthropologists.

It might well be impossible to draw a line of demarcation that demonstrates where microanthropology ends and cross-cultural psychology begins. A crude distinction would see anthropologists as being more interested in differences between cultures, and how cultural distinctiveness manifests itself in various practices. Cross-cultural psychology also dwells upon cultural distinctiveness, but here the emphasis is often placed upon how an individual's distinctiveness is partially informed by cultural factors. Crudely put, anthropology tends to focus upon large cultural differences, and considers the origin, purpose, and unintended consequences of these gross cultural patterns. Cross-cultural psychology, on the other hand, tends to consider how culture effects the individual, and vice versa. Although the overlap between these adjacent disciplines is enormous. Perhaps a recent, formal definition of cross-cultural psychology would help.

> Cross-cultural psychology is the study of similarities and differences in individual psychological functioning in various cultures and ethnic groups. It attempts to discover systematic relationships between (a) psychological variables at the individual level, and (b) cultural, social, economic, ecological, and biological variables at the population level. Researchers in the field examine the individual's actual experience of these population variables as they change. (Kagitcibasi and Berry 1989, 494)

One can see in this definition of cross-cultural psychology a strong concern for how large differences between cultures actually find their way into the psychological world and the actions of individuals. This tendency to study cultural influences as they act on the individual took an important turn with Triandis' (1972) work on subjective culture. It is not as if each of us has been dropped into some monolithic culture, which then exerts its inexorable effects upon us. Rather, we are raised in a plurality of cultural subgroups, each exerting a multiplicity of influences upon us. For example, each of us belongs to a racial group, a socioeconomic group, a sex group, a religious preference, a political constituency, and so forth. The subjective culture of each of us is strongly influenced by the degree of contact we have with people and institutions that focus upon (or see the world in terms of) their own subcultural perspectives. This fact can be seen as the basis for the old saying "Show me your friends, and I'll tell you the kind of person you are." We are molded by the subjective culture of our reference subgroup.

Initially, a child is greatly influenced by the cultural milieu of his or her family. With maturation the influence of the family generally declines, relative to the potency of other subcultural groups such as the neighborhood, the schools, and society in general. Many of the classic struggles between parents and their children in adolescence and early adulthood come about as children espouse the values and beliefs of their subjective culture subgroup that conflict with the beliefs and values of their parents' subjective culture. Stated in the terms of this chapter, struggles for independence by adolescents and young adults represent cross-cultural struggles as much as do misunderstandings and conflicts among members of different religions, races, nationalities, and the like. The stories advocated by the subjective cultures of adolescents often clash with the storied perspectives held near-and-dear by their parents.

How Stories Constitute Subjective Culture

The claims of narrative (or story-telling) psychologists have become more strident of late. For example, Sarbin (1986) in referring to human psychology (and after explicitly exempting the part of psychology that deals with sensory physiology) makes the following remarkable claim: "So psychology is narrative" (8). What part of psychology, then, is narrative in nature according to Sarbin? Almost everything of interest! Or consider again Mair's (1988) position that you saw earlier in this chapter.

> Stories are habitations. We live in and through stories. They conjure worlds. We do not know the world other than as story world. Stories inform life. They hold us together and keep us apart. We inhabit the great stories of our culture. We live through stories. We are *lived* by the stories of our race and place. It is this enveloping and constituting function of stories that is especially important to sense more fully. We are, each of us, locations where the stories of our place and time become partially tellable. (Mair 1988, 127)

At a very early age, children pepper their parents with a seemingly endless barrage of questions. Questions generally fit the following generic form: How can I understand (or make sense of) these puzzling aspects of my experience? Careful parents not only try to provide concrete answers to their child's questions, but they also strive to point them toward the general frames of reference (such as science, social customs, religion, cultural history, etc.) that make claims regarding meaning in our lives. For example, a child's simple question of "How did the world start?" could be answered either by summarizing Genesis or by offering a thumbnail sketch of Big Bang Theory. One answer offers a frame of meaning that sees the Bible as the Good Book; the other response suggests that Stephen Hawking's (1988) *A Brief History of Time* might be a good book. Both stories might be true (i.e., might actually have occurred), and the relative validity of the two stories depends upon the perceived plausibility of the two frames (science and religion) to each listener.

Lee Cronbach (1982) reminds us that "Validity is subjective rather than objective: The plausibility of the conclusion is what counts. And plausibility, to twist a cliché, lies in the ear of the beholder." (108). And while I suspect that you, Cronbach, the Pope, and I all have rather strong preferences for one of those frames (the scientific or the religious) over the other, I doubt that we'll ever all agree on the proper interpretive lens. Since a dissertation on epistemology is usually lost on a three-year-old, most parents usually answer the question with "God made the world" or "A long time ago there was a big explosion." But most three-year-olds (or at least my three-year-olds) would find either answer less than complete, coherent, and comprehensive. And so, question number 2 would be a novice story-teller's attempt to get me to tell the whole story (either of science or of religion) within which my first answer makes some degree of sense. Nine hundred ninety-eight questions-and-answers later, our neophyte narrativist might have some rudimentary grasp of either the culture of science or the culture of religion.

Parents aren't the sole source of stories—even for very young children. Beginning at a very early age, most American children watch many hours of cartoons each week. Cartoons tell stories ranging in length from 11 minutes (one must leave 8 minutes per half hour for commercials) to several hours (feature-length cartoons). Even at two or three years of age, children are entranced by cartoon stories, and they often try to explain the meaning or themes of the cartoon plots to their parents. Because children's thinking is more fluid than adult thought, the "impossibility" of cartoon plots does not often bother children. Adults are more constrained by proper notions of time, space, and causality, and thus prefer that the stories they seriously entertain be more "rational," "realistic," or "believable" than are cartoons. But children are far less discriminating in their fascination with stories. Tell, read, or show them a children's story, and you have their attention—often for longer than you had thought their attention-span could endure. Only later (at four, five, and six years of age) do children typically concern themselves with weighty discriminations, like which stories (and characters) are "real" and which are "pretend."

Finally, one should not think of cartoons as portraying only silly or superficial story lines to children. On three successive Saturdays "Alf Tales" presented *The Legend of Sleepy Hollow*, *Peter Pan*, and *Romeo and Juliet* to my children. Similarly, my childrens' favorite Walt Disney videocassettes are *Cinderella*, *Sleeping Beauty*, and *Pinocchio*. Such classics play out the eternal conflicts of good versus evil, issues of life and death, as well as the role of love and hate in human interactions (Bettelheim 1976). This is psychologically heavy material packaged in a medium that is attractive to very young children. The Jungian Hillman (1975) says that we are motivated, not by reason or by reinforcement, but by *fantasy*—the images and myths with which we have grown up. Jungians feel that many of the story elements that we live by are buried in our unconscious and are linked to the great myths that have captured the experience of the whole human race over eons of time.

Even if all members of a society told themselves exactly the same stories, the meaning and implications of these stories for different members of the society would not be the same. This is because there are many roles described in any story, and each of us must choose which role we will play in a story. Take *Romeo and Juliet* for example. Our sex could immediately eliminate half the roles offered as viable options. Further, one's age might suggest whether a "star-crossed lover" or one of their parents represents the most relevant role for us to fill. But here the literature in cross-cultural psychology might shed some light on this process.

Kagitcibasi and Berry (1989), in a recent review of cross-cultural psychology, claim that "Cross-cultural psychology, like many other branches (of psychology), still lacks, and badly needs, a conceptual framework" (495). But Brislin (1988) indicates how it is that people know what are the relevant roles for them in stories. He suggests that, "the four concepts of class, ethnicity, culture and race are social categories (Gardner, 1985) that *people use to think about themselves and others and to make decisions about their behavior*" (174–75, emphasis added). All stories offer a multiplicity of roles. Cross-cultural concepts direct us to the roles that are especially important to us in stories. For example, the film *Cry Freedom* had two protagonists: a white newspaper editor and a black antiapartheid advocate, both of whom lived in South Africa. The story was about friendship, oppression, and the sacrifices one makes to live out his or her values. Brislin (1988) suggests that race might serve to direct some of us to identify more closely with the black activist, whereas others of us would be more inclined to identify with the white newspaper editor. And whereas the movie clearly exalts friendship and resistance to oppression, it is instructive to inquire about what happens to people when they speak out against oppression (at least in this particular morality tale). Imagine that you identified with the black activist—he was brutally tortured and murdered by the police. The white editor's efforts met with a rather different ending—he wrote a book about his friend, which won a Pulitzer Prize that was later made into a movie, *Cry Freedom*. So after seeing that movie, will people be more likely to speak out against oppression? It depends.

Life—The Stories We Live By

Psychopathology—Stories Gone Mad

Psychotherapy—Exercises in Story Repair
If we have learned anything from the cognitive revolution in psychology, it is that the things that occur between one's ears are critically important in the genesis of human actions. There is a fair amount of disagreement as to how the hardware of the brain interacts with the software of the mind. And there is a great deal of disagreement as to which analogy is most appropriate to describe the various processes of cognition. That is, is thought best understood as TOTEs (Miller, Galanter, and Pribrim 1960), scripts (Schank and Abel-

son 1977), possible imagined future selves (Markus and Nurius 1986), stories (Mair 1988), or any of a handful of other possible models? Beyond these disagreements, one thing is clear—psychology once again appreciates the importance of mind and thought.

If one considers thinking as story-telling, and if one sees cross-cultural differences as rooted in certain groups entertaining differing stories and roles within stories, then one might see some examples of psychotherapy as interesting cross-cultural experiences in story repair.

Have you noticed that therapy usually begins with an invitation to the client to tell his or her story? Therapists have favored ways of phrasing their readiness to hear the client's tale, such as "Can you tell me what brings you here?" or "How can I be of help to you?" or "What seems to be the problem?" Clients generally know that these invitations do not request the telling of one's complete life story. Thus, we rarely hear replies like "I was born on June 8, 1948 in Bayonne, New Jersey, to John and Margaret Howard." Rather, clients understand that their task is to tell the part of their life story that appears most relevant to their presenting problem. Thus, one hears appropriate beginnings like "While I've always been a bit shy and withdrawn, since the breakup of my engagement last year I have been completely unable to . . ." or "I never worried too much about my weight, but since coming to college I've put on . . ." or "Drinking and socializing were always a large part of my job in sales. While I always drank a lot, I could always handle it. But lately. . . ."

In the course of telling the story of his or her problem, the client provides the therapist with a rough idea of his or her orientation toward life, his or her plans, goals, ambitions, and some idea of the events and pressures surrounding the particular presenting problem. Over time, the therapist must decide whether or not this problem represents a minor deviation from an otherwise healthy life story. Is this a normal, developmentally appropriate adjustment issue? Or does the therapist detect signs of more thoroughgoing problems in the client's life story? Will therapy play a minor, supportive role to an individual experiencing a low point in his or her life course? If so, the orientation and major themes of the life will be largely unchanged in the therapy experience. But if the trajectory of the life story is problematic in some fundamental way, then more serious, long-term story repair (or rebiographing) might be indicated. So, from this perspective, part of the work between client and therapist can be seen as life story elaboration, adjustment, and/or repair. Unfortunately, our therapeutic efforts are not uniformly successful.

An extensive literature has developed that demonstrates the importance of the therapist–client match upon therapy outcome. The search for "the important matching variable" has proven frustrating. Research has at times shown the importance of client–therapist match on the dimensions of race (Sue 1988); social class (Carkhuff and Pierce 1967); sex (Tanney and Birk 1976); cognitive style (Fry and Charron 1980); personal constructs (Land-field 1971); conceptual level (Stein and Stone 1978); personality variables (Dougherty 1976); complementarity of therapist–client needs (Berzins 1977); and personal epistemologies (Lyddon 1989). One thing is clear, however, getting a good client–therapist match is an important factor in therapy.

Many therapists conduct telephone interviews with clients prior to an initial therapy session, and intake interviews are standard operating procedure in many agencies. Therapists are attuned to issues that suggest whether or not they represent the optimal therapeutic resource for a particular client. Thus, referrals early in treatment (or even before it begins) often represent shifts to pairings that represent better client–therapist matches on critical dimensions. For example, if a client's story involves fundamental religious beliefs or problems due to childhood sexual abuse, I know therapists who are uniquely well equipped to help people with such problems—while I am ill prepared to help (and uncomfortable with) such life stories.

Recall Mair's (1988) point that "Stories are habitations." It is a fact that many people currently live in fundamental religious construals of their lives. That the stories of fundamentalists represent quite different habituations than the story in which I dwell is also a fact. The salient professional issue for me is whether I can wholeheartedly enter into a fundamentalist world-view. Can I be effective in helping a client to effectively rewrite his or her story while still remaining within the fundamentalist story line, if that is what the client so desires. Since others are more skilled than I in moving through the fundamentalist religious life world, I feel that I am ethically bound to let the client know that such specialists exist and that his or her best interests might be served by engaging such a specialist. Finally, I would no more engage a fundamentalist in therapy in order to move him or her out of a fundamentalist worldview than I would applaud a nonfeminist's efforts to undermine a feminist's belief system in therapy. After all, who died and left me to be God? Only an Enlightenment thinker would have the hubris to see a fundamentalist, or feminist, or any other cultural frame, as inferior to their own story of reality. All such instances of cultural elitism are distasteful to thinkers of a Romanticist temper.

We might also reconsider Mair's (1988) point about the influence of culture on our stories and lives, "We inhabit the great stories of our culture. We live through stories. We are *lived* by the stories of our race and place. . . . We are, each of us, locations where the stories of our place and time become partially tellable" (127). I am a creation of middle-class, American culture of the latter half of the twentieth century. I am also strongly influenced by the cultures of psychology and higher education (see Howard 1989). If I can see and understand the world at all, it is through spectacles colored by the worldviews of the cultural times and institutions in which I have dwelled. This is my world—the world I understand and operate within best. But other worlds are not completely opaque to me. I spent a brief moment in black South Africa in *Cry Freedom*; I visited Ireland at the turn of the twentieth century as I listened to stories at the knee of my Irish grandmother; Dostoyevski showed me a snapshot of nineteenth-century Russia in *Crime and Punishment*; and my wife has helped me to understand what it is like to be a woman in a male-dominated society. Empathic experiencing is perhaps the psychotherapist's greatest aid in escaping our inevitable limitations in understanding people from different cultures, races, belief systems, sexes, places, and times.

Beutler and his colleagues (Beutler 1981; Beutler, Clarkin, Crego, and Bergan 1990) speak of a "convergence of values phenomenon" that occurs in therapy. Treatment is experienced as effective when the participants begin with somewhat different perspectives, but close the gap between them as therapy progresses. Therapy might be seen as a cross-cultural experience where two life stories come together with each life-trajectory being altered somewhat by the meeting. This image recalls William James's insight,

> We are spinning our own fates, good and evil, and never to be undone. Every smallest stroke of virtue or of vice leaves its never so little scar. . . . Nothing we ever do is, in strict scientific literalness, wiped out. (James 1890, 130–31)

We are in the process of creating value in our lives—of finding the meaning of our lives. A life becomes meaningful when one sees himself or herself as an actor within the context of a story—be it a cultural tale, a religious narrative, a family saga, the march of science, a political movement, and so forth. Early in life we are free to choose what life story we will inhabit—and later we find we are lived by that story. The eternal conflict of freedom versus destiny is revealed in the old Spanish proverb:

Habits at first are silken threads—Then they become cables.

The next two chapters analyze two types of extremist stories—perfectionism and maximization—that have become overly popular at the close of the twentieth century in Western societies. Because we are not yet liberated from the grip of such environmentally toxic belief systems, my analysis of perfectionism is offered in an educational story where readers are presented with both sides of the " perfectionism-as-a-virtue" versus "perfectionism-as-pathology" debate. With this literary style, each reader should naturally gravitate toward the side he or she believes to be "the correct one." By doing so, I hope each reader can assess his or her belief with respect to value of perfectionism.

CHAPTER FOUR

~

The Perfect Class

Being excellent does not require being perfect.

—Henry James

There must be a million ways to prepare to teach a psychology class. It's twenty minutes till class starts. What will we cover? I lean back in my chair and gaze out my office window on the North Quad. . . .

"Okay, gang. Get quiet. Listen up." I began. "Today we tackle the most difficult topic in this class. Anybody want to take a guess at what it is?"

As the conversations and fidgeting slowly subsided, the room became ever more quiet.

"Drugs and alcohol?" a voice in the back asked.

"Nope," I replied.

"Sex and AIDS?" a girl offered.

I shake my head negatively and continued to wait.

"Religion?" a third student volunteered.

"Nope," I responded.

"Homosexuality?" was offered, and then immediately dismissed.

"All of these topics are real simple in comparison with the topic I have in mind for today. Think about it! Who in here is pro drug abuse? Who is completely opposed to sex? Or who wants to advocate for AIDS? All of these topics have obviously right and wrong positions."

A few students acted as if they were seriously mulling over endorsing one or more of the inappropriate options, but it was clear that their indecision was meant as a joke. I pause, then continued. "No, the topic I have in mind for today is much more controversial than those issues. Instead of telling you what the problem is, let me give you an example of how fundamentally you and I disagree on this topic. Tell me, how many of you want to get an A in this class?"

Every student pauses, as the query had all the earmarks of a trick question. I then fill the silence, "Well, that makes my job easier. If no one in here wants an A, I'll see to it that no one gets an A. Now I only have to decide who gets the B's, C's, D's, and F's. Nervous laughter by some and a few shouts of protest by others accompanied the rush of hands to express their hope of obtaining an A. "So everyone here wants an A," I summarize.

"Not everyone," Brian Selman says softly. "I didn't raise my hand."

"So that means you don't want an A, Brian? If I told you exactly what you needed to do to get an A—you wouldn't care to do it?"

"No, sir," the linebacker replied. "I'd do it. I just mean that I almost never get A's in my classes so I don't expect to get an A in this one. Especially since it's football season. . . ."

"I understand that, Brian. But that's not exactly the question I asked. Suppose I told you all of the things you needed to do to get an A—and they would all be things you are able to do. Would you do them in order to get an A? Would you do that work for an A?"

"Oh!" Brian replied hurriedly. "Then I would do it. Of course, I would."

"Why?" I asked.

The silence was deafening. Students shifted uncomfortably in their seats, not because they didn't know the answer, but because they couldn't grasp the point of the question. After many puzzled looks and unknowing grins, a typically quiet girl raised her hand barely to shoulder height. When my eyes met hers, she spoke softly.

"Why would we work to get an A? Is that the question?"

"That's precisely the question," I said emphatically.

"Isn't that what we're here for? Isn't that why we've agreed to pay a really high tuition? I don't understand the question. Isn't that what we're supposed to be doing here? Are you telling us *not* to study for your class?"

"No. Not at all," I replied. "If anyone cares to study for this class—please feel free to do so. And if anyone gets an A in the course—that won't bother me."

I responded to the students' puzzled looks with teasing smiles. After a pause, I added, "I just find it hard to believe that *all* of you are enthralled with the content of a course that you didn't choose to take. I mean, none of you requested this course, you were all forced to take it. You had to take a University Seminar, and the First Year of Studies assigned you to take my course on the Psychology of Healthy Lifestyles. And so it's stunning to me that when I ask, 'Who is willing to work for an A in this course?' I find that *everyone* is willing to do so. That's really sick!!"

Most students laughed at the thought of a psychologist labeling students who work hard to get good marks as pathological. Unfortunately, this psychologist was dead serious: "I'm not kidding. You guys are so brainwashed into getting good marks that you don't recognize it as a screwup when you try to get all A's."

After twenty seconds of stunned silence and perplexed looks, Tim went for the bait: "Okay, professor! I'll bite. What's better than all A's?"

"A few A's, a few B's, maybe even a C, and a life!"

"What are you saying? All work, no play makes Notre Damers dull boys and girls?"

"Exactly and not quite," I replied. "If you're working frantically *because* you want all A's then you'll not only become dull, you'll eventually be disappointed with your education and perhaps even with your life. That part of your answer I agree with completely. The part of your answer that I might take issue with is the implication that it is too much work that constitutes the problem. In fact, some of the hardest working people I know are among the happiest and healthiest people I know. So hard work per se is not the problem. It's whether you're working hard *because* you are genuinely passionate about your work—because it is *your* work—or whether you are working frantically at what someone else tells you to do."

"So the problem is whether you're following your true dream or someone else's dream for you—like something your parents want you to do," Anita offered.

"Exactly. But, unfortunately, our American educational system does a terrible job of helping kids find out what they are passionate about. We tell *you* what courses you should take, and then we wonder why your interest in most courses is only lukewarm. Then whatever effort we get from students is targeted toward avoiding the dreaded B's and C's. Often the only real passion we teachers see is from those crazy fanatics who are hell-bent on graduating from Notre Dame with a perfect 4.0 grade point average."

"Are you really that disappointed with us, professor?" Anita asked.

"No, I'm not, Anita. In fact, it's because I'm so pleased with your work so far that I'm crazy enough to attack a topic this fundamental to your belief system. Even if I present my ideas perfectly, most people will reject them as crazy—and perhaps dismiss me along with the ideas. But I've decided to lay out my beliefs on this topic because a few of you have convinced me that you are capable of questioning some fundamental assumptions of our society. So here goes.

"Several years ago two kids in California dropped out of school to build computers. Their names were Jobs and Wozniak. Another kid began to write the software that allows virtually all computers to run. Who am I talking about and where am I going with this?"

The sea of faces seemed universally perplexed by the challenge of responding to both an easy and an impossible question. Finally, Tim raised his hand and began slowly, "Well, Bill Gates is the easy answer. As to the hard question, all I'll say is that I really can't believe you've come to praise the Bitch Goddess Success."

I was initially startled by Tim's response. Then I smiled, as I recognized William James's phrase for "the sickness that lies at the heart of the American spirit"—Americans' worship of the Bitch Goddess of Success. I walked over to Tim's desk, chuckled, and whispered a reply that only Tim could hear easily: "No, friend. I come to bury the bitch."

"Great!" Tim barked. "But why use billionaires as examples? You're never gonna convince us that they are *un*successful."

"I'm not gonna try to convince you that they are *un*successful—they are very successful in my eyes. So are Mother Teresa, Albert Schweitzer, Tom Dooley, and John D. Rockefeller."

"Rockefeller just doesn't seem to fit with that last group," a voice from the back of the room announced. I was embarassed because I should have known his name—but didn't.

I responded: "He fits perfectly well, if only we were able to be money-blind. A racist is a person who can't be color-blind, and the sickness at the soul of our educational system has a lot to do with the fact that we can't be money-blind. We find it hard to imagine success without money, and, similarly, how can earning lots of money be failing?"

"We should act as if money doesn't matter?" a faceless voice from the back of the class queried.

"Absolutely not!" I replied. "An old Spanish proverb correctly observes, 'If money be not thy slave—it will be thy master.' We need to watch our money—and most importantly, our spending—like a hawk! Money is an important *means* to a happy, successful, and productive life. Unfortunately, for too many people, money is an 'end' not a 'means to an end' in their lives. We learn how to make lots of money in order to have the freedom to do what's important in our lives. But when people earn 'enough' they don't stop working for money. No matter how much money they have, it's never enough. So people spend their lives as slaves to making ever more money. Rarely do people say, 'I now have enough money. Now I'll turn my attention toward what is really important in my life.'

"Are you saying that if we make money at something, it can't be an important activity?"

"Not at all. I make a decent living teaching at Notre Dame, and I think it's important work. I also listed Gates, Jobs, Wozniak, and Rockefeller as successes, and they made serious money."

I walked to the desk, picked up a book, and said, "This is a book on the biology and psychology of altruism entitled *Unto Others*. My last example of a successful life is a nameless biologist—or perhaps it's a group of biologists—who are responsible for the following, fascinating bit of knowledge." I then read from the book.

> To see why evolutionists cannot resist talking about altruism, consider the trematode parasite *Dicrocoelium dendriticum*, which spends the adult stage of its life cycle in the liver of cows and sheep. The eggs exit with the feces of the mammalian host and are eaten by land snails, which serve as hosts for an asexual stage of the parasite life cycle. Two generations are spent within the snail before the parasite forms yet another stage, the cercaria, which exits the snail enveloped in a mucus mass that is ingested by ants. About fifty cercariae enter the ant along with its meal. Once inside, the parasites bore through the stomach wall and one of them migrates to the brain of the ant (the subesophagal ganglion), where it forms a thin-walled cyst known as the brain worm. The other cercariae form thick-walled cysts. The brain worm changes the behavior of the ant, causing it to spend large amounts of time on the tips of grass blades. Here the ant is more likely to be eaten by livestock, in whose bodies parasites may continue their life cycle. This is one of many fascinating examples of parasites that manipulate the behavior of their hosts for their own benefit. For our purposes, however, the example is interesting because the brain worm, which is responsible for putting the ant in the path of a grazing animal, loses its ability to infect the mammalian host. It sacrifices its life and thereby helps to complete the life cycle of the other parasites in its group. It is hard to resist calling this kind of behavior altruistic, even if the parasite doesn't think or feel anything about its fate.

Closing the book, I smiled and asked, "Can anyone tell me why I made this unknown biologist my last example of success?"

That anonymous voice from the back of the room ventured an opinion, "Because you wanted to gross us out?"

"No, that was an unintended, positive outcome," I chuckled.

The voice continued, "Seriously, is it because no one would go into that disgusting line of research with the thought that they could make a lot of money at it?"

"Yep," I smiled. "That's my hunch. I'm guessin' that this biologist began to study this trematode parasite—perhaps in graduate school—and the more he or she learned about it, the more perplexed and fascinated the biologist became. Perhaps it became the biologist's dissertation topic. In which case, the person would have spent a year or two working on this parasite pretty much full time."

"Isn't that like getting money for the work?" the nameless face in the back of class queried. "You make more money once you get a Ph.D."

"That's correct. Do you think I'm opposed to making money? Don't you know that most of your tuition dollars go toward paying faculty salaries? I'm not a wealthy man, so if Notre Dame stopped paying salaries, I'd have to find work somewhere else. What I'm suggesting instead, is that if you *fix* your eyes on making money, you might miss your passion in life. This biologist found his or her passion in life in a most unusual place—a lowly parasite. But here's the amazing thing—by following his or her passion, we learned something fascinating about the biological basis of altruism. I think that the biologist was probably rather surprised by the altruistic behavior of that brain worm. The biologist wasn't setting out to prove that there is a biological basis for altruism—much more likely he or she was simply trying to understand the life cycle of this strange little parasite."

"So you want us to choose our passion over money?" Anita asked skeptically.

"No! It's not an either/or choice," I replied emphatically. "If you follow your passion, you'll be so good at what you're doing that the money will follow. I believe that Bill Gates and Steve Jobs make obscene amounts of money *because* they are following their passions. But if someone else got into computer hardware or software *because* they wanted to make lots of money, not because they loved these areas, they wouldn't have been nearly as good at their work as were Gates and Jobs. And you know what happens to mediocre competitors in the business world—they get eaten alive. So, follow your passion and you'll be good at what you do. Follow money and it's unlikely you'll find what you are passionate about. And here's my last point—I can't prove it, but I think it's true—in the long run you'll actually make more money by following your passion than by following money. But even if that last point is not true, you'll make enough money, and you will definitely be much happier with your life and career if you follow your passion."

I suddenly realized that I had lapsed into a speech, when I really wanted to lead a discussion. "Hey, who put me up on that soapbox?" I kidded. "Tell me, what do you people think about what I said?"

Time passed slowly until Anita wondered aloud, "I get the money and passion part, but why is somebody messin' up if they get all A's?"

The temptation to lecture was almost irresistible. Still, a psychologist sometimes has to stick to his game plan. "Good question! Who can begin to answer it?"

"A's are like money." Tim began without even raising his hand. "Spend all your time working for all A's and you won't have any time left to find your passion—or is it that you won't have the energy left to find your passion?"

"Both," I replied. "Suppose our imaginary biologist simply memorized that the trematode parasite *Diocrocoelium dendriticum* is found in the liver of cows and sheep—because she or he thought that was all that was needed for the test. Then that person could spend the rest of the evening memorizing other biology facts that might also be on the test. Or he or she could be using the extra time to study for tests in calculus, theology, sociology, or literature—to maximize the chances of getting all A's. Instead, the passionate learner hops on the Internet and burns the remainder of the evening learning everything there is out there about *Diocrocoelium dendriticum*. A few months of this and the budding biologist has a report card full of B's and C's, a passion for an organism, and the start of a brilliant career."

"Wait a minute," Mr. Anonymous announces. "Becoming an expert on a liver-lovin' parasite, while pullin' down B's and C's represents a brilliant career?!? I don't think my dad and most med school admissions boards would agree."

"Write a long letter to the world's leading scholar in bovine parasitology and I'll bet you get a fellowship to study for a Ph.D. in biology. Perhaps your father has his heart set on you going to med school, but he'll get over it. After all, whose life is it? And the world will take a passionate parasitologist over an uninspired doctor any day."

Tim could contain himself no longer. "I can see why this biologist's career and life might be more satisfying when she or he follows their passionate interests, but how can you say the biologist is more successful than a Bill Gates? Think of the jobs Gates created, the money he's made, the power, the fame. You still don't even know this biologist's name—while everybody knows who Bill Gates is."

"Great comment, Tim. You've now hit the point where this analogy breaks down. Bill Gates was so successful *because* he was also following his passion.

Initially, he was following his interest in computer software, not success and money. I'll bet there were dozens of Bill Gates–types who also were following their passion for computer operating systems who were not nearly as success-ful as Gates. Who cares?! If they were following their passion, and if they made enough money to have a decent life, that's success in my book. All of these people—no matter how little money they made—were successful in my book."

"Getting back to someone who gets all A's being a screw-up. . . ." Anita laughed.

I corrected her gently, "Getting all A's per se isn't the screw-up. Failure is overworking in order to get all A's, or not giving sufficient time to topics you have a passionate interest for *in order to* study for something you could care less about. Those are the times when pressure to succeed—whether inter-nally or externally generated—causes us to screw-up."

"Are you telling me that you don't get upset if your kids bring home bad grades?" queried that person in the seat of the unknown student.

"That's exactly what I'm saying. My boys are in junior high and they are both very bright. The older one, John, is dyslexic. His typical grade is a B and he gets about equal numbers of A's and C's. He works pretty hard in school (the teachers say) and he does enough homework to satisfy me."

"So what's he passionate about?" Brian wondered.

"Basketball, rap music, and his social life. Nothing academic yet, if that was your question. But that's fine with me for now. He's a pretty typical 13-year-old."

"And you never hassle him about school?" Brian asked incredulously.

"Rarely," I replied. "Sometimes he doesn't do any work in a subject. Or he might get a bad conduct report from school. Then I'm on his case. That's when I see to it that his social life goes into the deep freeze. But he's always back on track in two to three days. Greg, my younger son, has an easier time academically. He gets mostly A's, an occasional A minus, and once in a blue moon, a B. He doesn't study near as much as his older brother, but then again, he doesn't need to."

"What's he passionate about?" Anita wondered.

"Fencing, basketball, and fantasy adventures—he loves this Brian Jacques guy."

"What did he get his B in?" someone asked.

"Religion," I replied. "Greg said his teacher was a jerk who wanted him to memorize stupid stuff. I made Greg show me his religion book and his test. Then I made him give me his views on those topics. Since I thought Greg's theology was superior to this teacher's, I told him the B was fine with me if it was fine with him."

"Did he keep on gettin' bad marks in religion?" Brian wondered.

"Nope. He went back to gettin' A's. Religion isn't hard for Greg—and he isn't opposed to gettin' A's. I honestly never asked him why his marks improved. Maybe the material in the next section was less objectionable to Greg. Or maybe his teacher became less jerky. . . ."

"Or maybe Greg sold out for the A," the anonymous one observed cynically.

I smiled and noted, "You don't know my Greg."

Tim needed a concrete example: "Let's get specific. Who in here should be working for a C rather than an A?"

"Good question," this psychologist replied. "Let's analyze your situation, Tim. What's your major?"

"Premed," Tim replied to the groans of several students.

"Doctors ought to be interested in the psychology of healthy lifestyles. Do you enjoy this class and its readings more than your other classes—like Calc and Orgo?"

Tim's "Get serious" was met with gales of laughter.

"Sorry, Tim," I teased. "You're not a good candidate for a C. I guess you'll have to settle for an A in this course."

As his colleagues gave him good-natured grief, Tim tried to make the best of his verdict. "It's a dirty job, but somebody's got to do it."

"Maybe I ought to work for a C," a quiet girl volunteered. Since this was the first time she had volunteered a response all semester, I was very pleased she'd spoken up.

"Why did you take this course?"

"My coach advised me to take it to fulfill my social science/history requirement."

"What sport?"

"Cross country."

"What's your major?"

"Engineering."

"What do you want to do with that degree?"

"Build computers."

"Wow," I observed. "You're sport is in season, you're taking a math- and science-heavy schedule. What do you do for a life?"

"I teach English to children at *Casa de Amistad*."

"Are you a freshman?"

"Yep."

"How did you get hooked up with *Casa* so quick?"

"My sister's a senior. She's tutored there for three years."

I threw up my arms in mock resignation, shouting, "What need have we for further evidence? The woman gets a C."

Everyone laughed except the engineer-in-the-making who wore an apprehensive smile as she waited for further clarification.

The anonymous guy in the back of the room pounced upon the opening like a trout on a May fly. "Clear out, honey. He just offered you a C for doing next-to-nothing. I'd take that offer in a heartbeat."

"Which is why I haven't offered a C to our loquacious friend in the back. This place would be dead as a morgue if he didn't come to class." I observed. "But I'm betting I could save myself an A by buying her off with a C now. This is a writing-intensive course with an essay final. Did you ever win an essay contest, distance lady?"

A slight nod of her head indicated she had.

"I'm thinking, high school salutatorian?"

Her arched eyebrow said, "Higher."

"Get out of town, lady!" I roared. "Better than the salutatorian? Take the C. I'll see you at the final, but the final is just a formality—you got the C. This lady's got A written all over her face. I feel like I'm saving myself an A."

"Take the C and get serious with your Playstation, honey," the voice of anonymity advised from the bowels of the back row. But the runner had no intention of quitting. Even in her worst nightmare, she pulls down a B plus. A C is completely unacceptable.

"Do you want me to take a C in your course, professor?" the runner asked skeptically.

"Depends," I replied. "Do you like this course more than your engineering and science courses?"

The freshman smiled sheepishly and replied, "This course is okay."

I translated, "That's a polite way of saying 'Not really.' Now tell me, does a runner plan out a marathon in advance?"

"Absolutely," she replied.

"When a marathoner hits the wall, that better not be the first time she entertained the possibility of its happening. Am I right?" I asked.

"Sure. You gotta have a strategy for every race."

"A strategy *and* contingency plans."

The runner nodded in agreement. "So if I hit the wall later this semester, and I have to back off on some subject, you'd recommend healthy lifestyles rather than calculus or electronics. Is that what you're saying?"

I beamed with approval. "Hey, if I sacrificed my physics and philosophy marks in order to protect my psychology grades, you can certainly sacrifice your psychology marks if your engineering courses need protecting."

"You took C's in physics and philosophy?" Brian Selman asked incredulously.

"Actually, I worked for C's. And while I didn't quite make them, I didn't fail either. But this was all before grade inflation struck. Back then D's weren't *that* bad. I mean, lots of guys got them. . . ."

"You got 'D's'!?" Brian asked in a voice that shouted 'Say it ain't so—Joe.'

"How'd you get in so much trouble that you had to work just to get D's?" Brian continued.

"I was taking 24 hours that semester."

"Twenty-four hours? That's impossible!"

"I had to. That's how many hours I needed to graduate. All I needed was D's to satisfy the area requirements—so I graduated."

"You were still satisfying area requirements when you were a senior? Did your adviser screw-up?"

"No, back then everyone was 'doing their own thing.' After all, it was 1969—people were a lot more laid-back about requirements then. I started out as a math major and then switched to psychology."

"Was math too much for you?" Mr. Anonymity editorialized.

"Nope. I always got great marks in math. But it just wasn't fun anymore. Even though my major was psychology, I taught high school math and physics."

"But didn't you get a D in physics?" Anita asked.

"Yep, but that was college physics not high school physics. Besides, physics was one of eight courses that I was taking, and I had no interest in it at the time. If I'd wanted to, I could have gotten a much better mark in physics. I was more interested in other courses."

"If you had no interest in physics, why did you teach it?" Anita persisted.

"Psychology wasn't taught in high school back then. If I wanted to teach, I had to teach math and science."

"How did teaching physics go?" Anita asked.

"Oh, I loved it. But after two years of teaching math and science I missed psychology. So I went to graduate school to get a Ph.D."

My eye caught the clock at the front of the room. I thought for a moment, then realized I needed to summarize, "Today college students seem much more concerned with their grades than we were thirty years ago. It's as if students today think that two or three bad grades will ruin your career."

"Well, won't it?" Anita asked.

"Nope," I replied. "But most people around here believe a few bad marks will. So my chances are small of convincing you that a handful of bad grades won't cripple your career. Before I go further, I need to correct a possible misconception. The main reason I am trying to destigmatize low marks is *not* so that you'll feel better when you get lower grades. Rather, I think students are not following their intellectual interests in the depth that they ought to *because* they are spreading themselves thin in order to get the highest possible grades in all areas. That's the screw-up I've been attacking. Follow your love, your genuine interests, and your passion. If you are working hard at something you love, forget about your overall GPA. Don't kill yourself trying to get all A's. Take B's and C's where you deem they are appropriate. See the extremism of wanting all A's as the mistake. Perfectionism is a sickness. Extremism, even in the service of a virtuous cause, is to be deplored by reasonable. . . ."

The cynic in the back was waving his hand frantically, "You're not this worked-up about GPAs. What are you really talking about?"

Because I had planned out the class, I knew the answer—*The absolutism of modern society is creating frantic, hollow people.* However, since I was trying my best to use a Socratic teaching method, I demured, "I'm not sure exactly what I want to say, but you wanna' know what really pisses me off? At next Saturday's football game, about eight times, the NBC cameras will show the Notre Dame student section. And there'll be about twenty jackasses, mugging for the camera, shaking their index finger, screaming, 'We're number one! We're number one!' What a bunch of jerks! They are such an embarrassment to us. Those idiots remind me of those dogs you see in the back window of cars—with their heads on springs—if they could talk, I guarantee the dogs would be saying, 'We're number one! We're number one!'"

As the roars of laughter subsided, the blabbermouth in the back tried to rouse the rabble, "Let's tell the truth in our cheers. 'We really stink! We really stink!'"

"We don't stink!" I bellowed. "We're a winning team! We're 4 and 3 for christsakes!"

"Then what should we say to the NBC cameras?" Anita asked softly.

"We might try telling the truth," I whispered in reply. "But I wager that our commitment to extremism and perfectionism keeps most of us from even *knowing* the truth—let alone speaking it."

I hurried to the front of the classroom and wrote "We're __ __ __." I then turned to the class and announced, "Everybody write down their answer to next Saturday's *truthful* pregame chant. Do it now! You have to tell the truth in four words or less. I'm gonna' call on people, so everybody's got to come up with something. We're __ __ __. Tell the truth about our football team."

After a minute's wait I began pointing at students who each offered their versions of truthful chants. I then responded to each 'Truth.'

"We're really desperate."

"Yep."

"We're struggling."

"Yep."

"We're still hoping for a major bowl."

"Unfortunately, our chances are slim and none. But that's a good one."

"I don't follow football. I can't come up with an answer."

"Okay."

"We're playing for next year."

"Perhaps."

"We're looking for a new coach."

"I hope not."

"We're in disarray."

"Could be."

"I couldn't come up with anything."

"That's okay."

I sat on the desk and spoke slowly, "Most of those were true statements, but they really weren't true analyses of our football season thus far. Follow me on a thought experiment, if you would. Imagine we had the eleven coaches we face this year in a room before the season began. In a secret vote (for honesty reasons), they have to guess what our record for the season will be. They know our team well. They are all optimistic people who hope to beat us, but coaches who tend to underestimate their opponents don't last long in the profession. Brian, what record do *they* think we'll have? What's your guess?"

"I dunno. Eight and three maybe?"

"Yep."

"Tim, what do you think?"

"More like seven and four."

"That's what I guessed. We have a tough schedule, but not a backbreaker. We have good talent at every position. We are, however, very thin at running back, defensive line, and defensive back. While defensive line and running back have held up so far, we lost a starting cornerback and his replacement—a walk-on freshman—early in the season. If we give that new information to the eleven coaches, what do they guess? I think they'll say 5–6 or 4–7. And what do they think our record would be after our first seven games? I'd guess 2–5, 3–4, or 4–3! So I think a truthful chant for our team would *not* be 'We're number one!' That's just stupid. We should be chanting 'We're modestly successful!' or 'We're exceeding expectations.'"

The roars of laughter foresaw the nation's astonishment if Notre Dame's spring-head dogs were to chant, 'We're exceeding expectations,' in response to a 4–3 start. But the football players in class were ashen-faced.

"What's it like over in the Joyce Center these days, Brian?" I asked softly.

The linebacker shook his head in disbelief and muttered, "It's grim—really bad."

"It sure is, son," the psychologist replied. "The pressure is withering."

"So you think the disappointment and the pressure are uncalled for," Tim suggested.

"Absolutely," I replied.

"But isn't that a coaching strategy designed to make players hate losing?" Tim continued.

"And how effective is that strategy?" I countered.

"It might work sometimes," Tim offered.

"And I guarantee it fails sometimes," the teacher replied. "Bottom line is that nobody knows for sure which coaching strategies will work and which will blow up. I just hope that the coaching staff has the *capability* of responding to the enormous pressure that they're under either by passing it along to the players or by shielding the players from it completely. Then, at least, their actions would represent a *coaching* decision. If a coach is incapable of one or another of those responses, then I think we should fire the coach and get someone who has more coaching flexibility."

"But even if the coach could shield the players from the pressure, you'd allow him to dump it on them anyway?" Brian asked.

"Wow, this is complex," I replied. "Let me break down my answer into several parts. First, in a very few cases, for individual players, turning up the pressure represents both a good coaching decision(which is concerned primarily with wins and losses) and also a good psychological decision—and by that I mean to hell with wins and losses. What's best for this kid for the rest of his or her life (the sort of issues that good parents worry about)? Second, in perhaps an equal number of individual cases, while it might get more wins in the short run, turning up the pressure will also have negative long-term psychological effects. I can't prove that point, it's just my experience over the years as an athlete, psychologist, coach, and parent. Third, my experience at Notre Dame is that our teams are almost always under too much pressure—both internally and externally generated—to win. So turning up the pressure on the whole team is probably a bad coaching decision, and it is almost always a bad move for the student-athletes psychologically also. But, of course, all of this is unprovable, it's just my experience, and after all, who died and left me God?"

"But still," the cynic in the back row opined, "given what you just said, why shouldn't Notre Dame fire any coach who puts pressure on his or her athletes?"

"Remember, a moderate amount of pressure is often good. We're talking about putting extreme amounts of pressure on student-athletes. But there's also a fairness issue here that needs to be considered. Fairness to the coaches is also at stake. It's duplicitous for us to put extreme pressure on our coaches to win and then tell them they can't pressure student-athletes, if the coaches genuinely feel doing so will help them to save their jobs. Let's be fair about this. If we continue to squeeze coaches to win, there will be negative consequences on our student-athletes. It's only human nature. Just like if we continue to squeeze faculty to be excellent scholars for tenure, there will be negative consequences for undergraduate teaching—it's just human nature. And don't fall for the lines of rhetoric about what we do in the scholarship domain having no negative effects on teaching. Everything in the world of human affairs is interconnected. That's why it's so difficult to do the analyses about human lifestyles that we attempt in this class. My summary is that *until* we can tell coaches that their job security rests with an analysis of their coaching—where under some circumstances people have many more losses than wins but still are graded as effective coaches—*we* are wreaking bad coaching decisions on our student-athletes. Bottom line, we have to let coaches get some B's and C's in some classes, if we are to demand they get A's in the more important domains."

I turned toward the front of the class and was shocked, "Whoa. Look at the time. We've got to get out of here. Today's class was entitled 'The Dread Disease of Perfectionism: Theoretical Issues.' Our class on Friday will be 'Against the Dread Disease of Perfectionism: Treatment Strategies.' For anyone interested in getting an A, or an education in psychology. . . ."

"Or both?" came the voice from nowhere.

"Or both," I replied cheerfully. "You can write a preview paper. Think of paradoxes like Chinese handcuffs, or success through defeat, or 'it is in dying that we are born.' That sort of stuff. Okay? Write essays on how to defeat pressures toward perfectionism in your lives."

Students were doing dozens of things—gathering books, staring blankly, nodding enthusiastically, whispering to one another, and the like. I needed one more minute, "Okay gang. Get quiet. Listen up. (Pause) For reaction papers to today's class, imagine the following scenario. Each of you grades me on today's class. What do you give me? A? B? C? D? F? We average those twenty grades and it comes out to a B plus. I yell 'B plus! That's a perfect class!' Write a reaction paper to that last sentence. Okay?"

Students headed for the door as the backrow-brain yelled, "Can we write a reaction paper on whatever we want to?"

I smiled resignedly and said, "Whatever! If it's wise, and about real-life issues, it's related to this class—so I guess you can do it. But I'd really like you to seriously try planning some losses into your lives. So please? Do it for me? Write about my perfect B plus."

I was jolted from my reverie by a delicate knock on my open door. It was our distance-running computer-engineer-in-the-making.

"I'm sorry to disturb you, professor," she began demurely.

"That's okay," I replied. "I was just preparing for class." I rubbed the sleep from my eyes and stretched as I rose from my chair.

Her quizzical look suggested she thought I might be joking. But she decided she'd better play it straight. "Class was supposed to start ten minutes ago. Should I tell the kids to wait for you?"

"Of course you should!" I bellowed as I fumbled to find my course folder. "Tell them to stay put. Today we're gonna have the perfect class."

CHAPTER FIVE

~

The Tragedy of Maximization

The ecology movement has now achieved sufficient maturity to identify the field's founding works. Among the most cited books are Rachel Carson's (1962) *Silent Spring*, Paul Ehrlich's (1968) *The Population Bomb*, E. L. Schumacher's (1973) *Small Is Beautiful*, and Aldo Leopold's (1949) *A Sand County Almanac*. Perhaps the single most important journal article for the movement is Garrett Hardin's (1968) *Science* paper on "The tragedy of the commons."

Hardin speaks of a shared public resource (public grazing land) that becomes decimated by overgrazing because each individual rancher might try to maximize his/her profit by grazing as many cattle on the commons as he or she could afford. Unfortunately, the public resource is soon destroyed through overuse, and all ranchers suffer tremendously. Hardin argued convincingly that a tragic consequence is virtually inevitable when sharing resources, as long as each person is intent on maximizing his or her own profits. The fading years of the twentieth century document the prescience and pervasiveness of Hardin's analysis (e.g., the decimation of certain Atlantic and Pacific fish stocks, the burning of the rainforests, the decline of our national parks, etc.) when individual self-interest comes into conflict with the common good. However, if the myopic pursuit of self-interest leads to tragedies, as Hardin suggests, why would rational humans continue to try to maximize their self-interest?

The Tragedy of Certain Self-Fulfilling Prophecies

In earlier times, the description of human nature fell largely to humanistic disciplines such as religion and philosophy. Over the last 200 years, the social sciences (e.g., psychology, sociology, economics, political science) have assumed even larger roles in characterizing humans' basic nature. While the social sciences initially held an array of visions of human nature, of late they seem to have grown more similar in their root metaphors for humans. Richard Herrnstein (1990) states this fact bluntly, "Not just economics, but all the disciplines dealing with behavior, from political philosophy to behavioral biology, rely increasingly on the idea that humans and other organisms tend to maximize utility, as formalized in modern economic theory. . . . The scattered dissenters to the theory are often viewed as just that—scattered and mere dissenters to an orthodoxy almost as entrenched as a religious dogma" (356).

Barry Schwartz (1986) in *The Battle for Human Nature* demonstrates how the notion of utility maximization in economics is transformed into reinforcement maximization in behavioral psychology, into maximizing the number of one's genes that make it into the next generation's gene pool in sociobiology, and so on. It's as if the social sciences are determined to convince humans that the "winners" in life are those who die with the largest bank accounts, those who have consumed the most pleasurable experiences, and those who have left the largest number of offspring. Nothing could be farther from the images of human nature and the good life articulated by thinkers of antiquity, such as Jesus, Mohammed, Confucius, Aristotle, Lao Tzu, and Buddha.

To the extent that people believe it is in their nature to maximize individual "goods," they will orient their lives toward the attainment of self-interested goals. Then, as each of us reflects upon the experience of our lives, we find that the maximization of our self-interest represents the most compelling explanation of our own nature and experience as humans. That we might have become a different type of person, had we entertained different beliefs about human nature and the good life, rarely tempers our sad conclusion about human motivation.

In our research, we social scientists often engage in the same circular, self-fulfilling prophecy. But here the self-deception is ironclad, as we imply that such "scientific, scholarly investigations" are objective, value neutral, and based only upon the bedrock of facts. We are wrong in implying that our findings are value neutral, but since it is often in our self-interest to maintain this self-deception, clearly seeing through to the assumptive biases in our beliefs will always be a daunting challenge.

The lie, that human nature demands that individuals maximize their self-interest, is particularly problematic for biological ecosystems. Economies, governments, businesses, and the like might work well with a fundamental assumption of the maximization of self-interest. However, Hardin's tragedy of the commons suggests that life in an overpopulated world of self-interested maximizers will be horrific. Unfortunately, it becomes clearer by the year that the twenty-first century will have precisely this nightmarish character. World population *increases* by 95,000,000 souls (and appetites also) each year—with no lessening of this yearly increase in the offing. And what is the fundamental worldview of the world's six billion humans? Because of the worldwide communications revolution, the consumerist, capitalist beliefs of the developed world are being broadcast to people everywhere. Free market capitalism represents a self-interested, maximizing belief system. Because both individuals and corporations are instructed to maximize their profits, the current credo has become "let no human *want* go unsatisfied." Madison Avenue produces the propaganda to multiply wants worldwide. Then the corporate world scrambles to make profits by satisfying consumers' geometrically expanding desires. While this strategy might make impeccable sense for individuals, businesses, economies, and governments—in the short run—it is doomed to failure in the long run because it is based upon ever-increasing material throughput (i.e., business activities that consume resources and produce wastes).

The trajectory of growth in the global human population can clearly be seen as a geometric (or exponential) trend when viewed over a long period of time—such as the last thousand years (see figure 1.1 in chapter 1). If the world and its resources were increasing geometrically, as is the world's population, the consumption of nonrenewable natural resources, and the creation of waste products, then this maximization fantasy might continue indefinitely. However, the biological and physical resources upon which life depends (e.g., potentially arable land, extractable hydrocarbons, fresh water, biologically diverse ecosystems) are all finite. While we can and should find ways to use these resources more efficiently, we live in a world of important physical and biological limits. Yet, we've adopted worldviews that rest upon dreams of geometric growth.

The reality is that the Western, free market capitalist system, that encourages the current geometric rates of increase in population, production, consumption, and waste generation, represents a terrifying, pyramid scheme. Eventually we will overwhelm our ecosystems, unless we change our beliefs and lifestyles. If data on per capita energy consumption worldwide remained constant over time, the slope of our energy consumption curve would be identical to the population curve in figure 1.1 of chapter 1. If per capita energy declined over time, the slope of the curve might be less steep than for the population graph above. Unfortunately, per capita energy consumption worldwide continues to increase, going from 1,090 kg. (oil equivalent) in the 1960s, to 1,175 in the 1970s, to 1,369 in the 1980s, and to 1,442 in the early 1990s (*World Development Report*, The World Bank). Thus, the trajectory for energy consumption is even more ominous than the curve for population in figure 1.1. A similar verdict is true for waste production, as carbon-based energy consumption is highly correlated with waste production. In fact, energy consumption is often used as a surrogate variable for waste generation in the ecology literature.

Reexamining Ancient Wisdoms

What are the worldviews that do not seek to maximize material throughput, and thus hold the possibility of fostering sustainable lifestyles in the twenty-first century? A theologian might note that many religions promote moderation, and thus tend to encourage earth-friendly lifestyles. For example, in *Small Is Beautiful* the economist E. L. Schumacher (1973) shows the intrinsically self-defeating characteristics of Western, maximizing, approaches to economics. He then offers a chapter entitled "Buddist Economics" that rethinks our most basic economic assumptions and offers alternative foundations based upon a Buddist belief system and notion of the "goods" in life. Material goods are to satisfy human *needs* (as opposed to "wants") and are never collected for the sake of becoming wealthy.

> The cultivation and expansion of needs is the antithesis of wisdom. It is also the antithesis of freedom and peace. Every increase of needs tends to increase one's dependence on outside forces over which one cannot have control, and therefore increases existential fear. Only by a reduction of needs can one promote a genuine reduction in those tensions which are the ultimate causes of strife and war. (Schumacher 1973, 31)

We'll consider Buddhist economics in greater depth in part III.

An examination of the New Testament reveals that Jesus lived a life that eschewed maximization, lavish consumption, and materialism at every turn.

When queried as to what would constitute success in life, He offered a story of lilies of the field who "neither spin nor toil" but who are unequaled by "Solomon in all his glory." Similarly, He noted that it is easier for a camel to pass through the eye of the needle than for a rich man to go to heaven. Like "Buddhist Economics," Jesus teaches a spiritual enlightenment that focuses our attention on a world that lies beyond our material world. Undue attachment to the things of this world represents a danger to the life of the spirit. Material possessions are not intrinsically bad. Rather, sin might result from being overly attached to material possessions, or by losing sight of spiritual goods, due to a myopic fixation on maximizing one's material possessions. In the Christian tradition, this form of maximization would represent a tragic mistake.

More generally, many indigenous cultures present ecologically appropriate worldviews that enjoin people against maximizing present consumption or wealth. For example, most native American cultures only hunted enough animals to satisfy their needs for food and clothing. Rather than simply maximizing short-term profit, the Sioux explicitly mandated that its leadership evaluate any action's impact upon the next seven generations of Sioux before initiating a policy change. *In the Absence of the Sacred* (Mander 1991) documents the systematic destruction of indigenous cultures worldwide by the spread of our dominant Western culture. Nonmaterialist worldviews represent a storehouse of alternative belief systems that might serve as partial templates for creating a nonmaterialist, nonconsumption-oriented vision of human nature. Western culture is thereby destroying the visions and values that might serve to temper its excesses. It is almost as if the maximization principle is systematically maximizing its chances of becoming the *only* vision of human nature. Almost thirty years ago Schumacher (1973) warned that "spiritual values" represented our only defense against the hegemony of the maximizing, economic vision.

> As a society, we have no firm basis of belief in any meta-economic values, and when there is no such belief the economic calculus takes over. This is quite inevitable. How could it be otherwise? Nature, it has been said, abhors a vacuum, and when the available "spiritual space" is not filled by some higher motivation, then it will necessarily be filled by something lower—by the small, mean, calculating attitude to life which is rationalized in the economic calculus. (Schumacher 1973, 109)

Edward Wilson (1992) in *The Diversity of Life* points out that we have just entered into the sixth great extinction period in the roughly 600-million-year history of the expansion of life on our planet. Unlike the five previous extinction periods, which were likely produced by nonhuman causes like asteroids or volcanoes, human activity represents the cause of our current crisis. The twin engines of ecological destruction are human overpopulation and overconsumption (i.e., living unsustainable lifestyles). Unless the human race soon curbs its numbers, and tempers its consumerist lifestyles, the fabric of life upon which our species depends will be badly (perhaps irreparably) ravaged.

If you think that our species would not be so stupid as to destroy the web of life that is required to sustain our very existence, consider this chilling fact. We know of no biological species that has voluntarily controlled its own numbers. Nature, "red of tooth and claw," has always stepped in to control population growth in all species. If we wait for nature to control us, it will likely occur through famine and regional wars over scarce resources—although we might instead be overwhelmed by our own waste products. Unfortunately, in the overpopulated world of the twenty-first century, billions of people might be sacrificed to bring our population back to sustainable levels. This loss of life will easily dwarf any other tragedy in human experience.

Hope for the Future

More than thirty years ago in *The Population Bomb*, Paul Ehrlich (1968) accurately foresaw the present population and ecological crises.

> In summary, the world's population will continue to grow as long as the birth rate exceeds the death rate; it's as simple as that. When it [the world's population] stops growing or starts to shrink, it will mean that either the birth rate has gone down or the death rate has gone up or a combination of the two. Basically, then, there are only two kinds of solution to the population problem. One is a "birth rate solution" in which we find ways to lower the birth rate. The other is a "death rate solution," in which ways to raise the death rate— war, famine, pestilence—find us. The problem could have been avoided by population control, in which mankind consciously adjusted the birth rate so that the "death rate solution" did not have to occur. (Ehrlich 1968, 34–35)

Interestingly, Ehrlich held out hope for a birth rate solution. He implied that, unlike all other species, human beings *might* voluntary choose to limit the size of our species' population. However, doing so is virtually impossible if we do not believe in some set of values higher than maximization principles. This is especially true if the alternative is for each of us to believe the sociobiologists' claim, that our role in life is to maximize the number of our genes that make it into the next generation's gene pool.

Human overpopulation is the most important issue for the underdeveloped world, where birth rates are extremely high. In the United States (and most other developed countries) our birth rate is close to the replacement rate of 2.1 children per family. For us, overconsumption of nonrenewable natural resources, and the subsequent overstressing of common waste sinks, represents our most important challenge. Specifically, the average American consumes sixteen times the energy (and produces sixteen times the waste) of the typical inhabitant of India. We are trapped within the most polluting production/consumption system in history. Thus, when we export our materialist, consumption-maximizing, free market system, we encourage people in other cultures to emulate our worst (ecologically speaking) habits. Americans' first challenge is to repair our free market, capitalist ways of doing business so that they become more earth-friendly [see Hawkin's (1993) *The Ecology of Commerce* and Howard's (1997) *Ecological Psychology: Creating a More Earth-Friendly Human Nature*]. The first step in this process is to replace some of our consumption-oriented, maximizing beliefs with perspectives that prize nonmaterialist values. Then we can set about the exciting challenge of retooling our free market system so that it does not attempt to maximize material throughput. The resulting system might then produce sustainable growth—progress that will not endanger the physical resources and the biological web of other life forms that supports our life on this planet.

Extremism in the Service of a Good Cause . . .

If we believe that humans are maximizers by nature, we are vulnerable to believing extremist positions in a variety of domains. For example, many people who claim to be Notre Dame fans will only be satisfied if we have an undefeated, national championship football team. Such people can give up on the team with its first loss (and are quoted in the student newspaper as doing so year after year after year). They are unwilling to "settle" for anything less than perfection (i.e., the maximum possible performance) from our team. The "Number 1 or nothing" crowd (and indeed all perfectionists) actually pride themselves on their "high standards" and on "being unwilling to settle for *mediocrity*." In reality, these attitudes might represent the single greatest obstacle to Notre Dame conducting a football program of which the university can be proud. Such extremist fans (in my judgment) work against the university's desire to be great in many domains—scholarship, teaching, athletics, service, faith, etc. Why do so many people endorse the "I only want the best (Number 1) for you (my spouse, my children, my university, etc.)" position, if it is as problematic and self-defeating as I imply?

Many of us are worn down by the complexity and unending demands of contemporary life. Consider only the social, political, and moral issues that we must confront. Each represents a complex labyrinth of issues, interests, and competing values, where experts—even after a lifetime of study of an issue—still violently disagree. How can the rest of us—whose energies are consumed in raising a family, shepherding a career, helping our parish, friends, relatives, etc.—form a defensible view on such thorny issues? A psychologically expedient solution is to declare oneself in favor of a few basic values (e.g., a free speech advocate, prodemocracy, anti-abortion, pro-social justice, a free market capitalist, a radical environmentalist, etc.) and then to simplify complex issues by viewing them through the conceptual lenses of our basic beliefs.

While the world presents itself to us as a complex tapestry of grays, endorsing one (or a few) basic value(s) can melt the complexity and make issues seem black and white. Doing so enables us to quickly determine our position on most issues. Recall that the history of scholarship in psychology repeatedly demonstrates that thinking in either/or dichotomies can prove unhelpful. In such instances, either/or frames might be replaced by both/and conceptualizations. Adopting both/and integrations (where our society tempts us to see issues in terms of either/or dichotomies) will make us less likely to fall into the traps of radicalism, fundamentalism, extremism, and maximization that stalk contemporary intellectual life.

One might see this entire book as an ode to the golden mean—a plea for moderation to oppose the idols of our radicalized age. I hope Notre Dame's football team has a very good year, but I believe it would be a mistake for any of us to take time, effort, or attention away from our educational, spiritual, and social missions to fanatically chase an undefeated season. Similarly, while it will be difficult for many to understand, I urge all to see the wisdom of becoming both a free willist *and* a determinist, an environmental activist *and* a free market capitalist, a pro-choice advocate *and* an anti-abortion advocate. These hot controversies would not have remained burning issues for so long if there was no truth or wisdom to be gleaned from either of the (presumed) polar opposites. The middle path, of extracting and integrating the best from both antagonists, seems to represent the wise course. I'll remind you of the motto that helps me to avoid some of the pitfalls of our overly radicalized age—Extremism, even in the service of a virtuous cause, is to be deplored by reasonable people. As I read the inspired writings of the ancients, they seem ripe with stories and principles that advocate wise moderation. Moderation is a virtue that is currently in short supply. Perhaps this is one cause of the many problems that haunt our troubled times.

Is extremism *always* bad? My colleague and friend Jeff Noethe offered the following helpful perspective, which I'll use to end this chapter.

Acceptable (or Balanced) Extremism
"Extremist" is a label applied to people who advocate or resort to "measures beyond the norm" (Dictionary.com). It is generally regarded as a negative label suitable for terrorists, racists, radical environmentalists, and the like, but it has also been applied to people who are now regarded as heroes, such as Gandhi, Malcolm X, Rachel Carson, and the American Revolutionaries of the 1700s.

This brings up an interesting question: Is some extremism *truly* justifiable? Or do we simply approve of extremism that works in favor of our own personal values, beliefs, and wants?

It would be convenient to claim that extremism is acceptable when grounded in some objective right, good, or truth. However, the road to establishing universally endorsed truths (or "goods") is (to say the least) daunting—and a problem frequently encountered by Enlightenment thinkers.

It would also be convenient to claim that extremism is acceptable when it is not grounded in fear, pride, or selfishness. However, humans are rarely willing to accept or admit that they are influenced by such emotions. People want to believe that they are free and that they have chosen a path that is clear and true. The net result of such human self-deception seems to be a stalemate in our efforts to determine universally agreed-upon values or truths.

The only remotely defensible rationale may be to claim that extremism is acceptable when grounded in a balanced (nonextreme) awareness. A balanced, pluralistic awareness is open, broad, thoughtful, and constantly questioning. It tries to carefully consider all the experiences and messages brought by life, including those that come from nature, logic, history, spirit, and even fear. Only by pursuing such balance can we avoid falling victim to the narrow, simplistic, or myopic perspective that leads to unjustifiable and unproductive forms of extremism.

Extremism versus Moderation
It is tempting to condemn all extreme actions as "unjustifiable and unproductive" and to encourage only more moderate actions as a vehicle of change. However, "moderate actions" are, by definition, anchored to and defined by the context of cultural norms within which they take place. If those cultural norms are part of the problem, then moderate actions may never promote real change.

Extreme actions are not inherently problematic. The real problem is a lack of balanced awareness. A narrow, simplistic, or myopic perspective rarely serves any positive end, but focused, uncompromising, or "extreme" actions can be a powerful tool for positive change, as long as they are not used blindly or narrow-mindedly. By condemning all people who act in an extreme manner, we effectively throw out the baby with the bathwater. Ironically, we also demonstrate our own lack of balanced awareness by accepting such a simplistic view of "extremists."

Unfortunately, extremist actions are often discouraged by cultural norms, even when those actions are grounded in a balanced awareness. Sometimes, the balanced awareness itself is condemned as extreme! This happens when cultural norms become rigid, defensive, and incapable of tolerating diversity of thought. History is ripe with examples of progressive thinkers (e.g., Galileo Galilei, Dietrich Bonhoeffer, Mohandes Gandhi, Rachel Carson) who were ridiculed, shunned, and even condemned, only to be vindicated at a later date (once cultural norms had changed). For some, vindication came too late.

As a result of cultural discouragement, balanced awareness and extreme action are often all too rare, especially in those cultures and times when they are needed most. Thus, we must be careful to remember that narrow-mindedness (unbalanced awareness) is our true enemy, not radical thoughts or extreme actions. To forget this simple truth is to condemn ourselves to a rigid, defensive, and intolerant existence.

Why Is Narrow-Mindedness So Common?

In a complex and demanding world, it is much easier for us to simplify, narrow-down, categorize, and stereotype the wealth of stimuli that we encounter. This process is quite natural for us, often even essential. But there are times when this essential process becomes warped, and we go to irresponsible and judgmental extremes of perception. Racism, sexism, and consumerism are all examples of what happens when perception becomes *too* focused or narrow.

In our modern, Western world, we too have fallen victim to a warped awareness. Generally speaking, we have become like spoiled children. We have no discipline, no honor, little desire for truth, and we process a whole menagerie of fears. We are selfish and lazy beyond measure, proclaiming every luxury to be a need and a right. We have even lost interest in achieving balanced awareness! In such a world, the occasional extreme action is likely to be misguided, yielding negative or destructive results, which can then be used as evidence to further invalidate the use of extreme actions.

With balanced awareness being such a rarity, perhaps it is best that we don't encourage extremism. After all, few (if any) seem qualified to wield such power!

Who is qualified to wield power and take "extreme" action? One answer to this question is provided by Deng Ming-Dao's (1983) description of the "Scholar Warrior":

> Skill is the essence of the Scholar Warrior. Such a person strives to develop a wide variety of talents to a degree greater than even a specialist in a particular field. Poet and boxer. Doctor and swordsman. Musician and knight. The Scholar Warrior uses each part of his or her overall ability to keep the whole in balance, and to attain the equilibrium for following the Tao. Uncertainty of the future inspires no fear: Whatever happens, the Scholar Warrior has the confidence to face it. (*Scholar Warrior*, 10)

The Scholar Warrior is dedicated to maintaining a balanced perspective and to living a life of strong actions. He or she is dedicated to learning, training, honor, compassion, and discipline. He or she also avoids simplistic thinking, quick judgments, careless actions, and the temptations of fear, pride, and selfishness. The Scholar Warrior is qualified to take extreme action, because all actions are taken with great mindfulness and responsibility.

If we are to justify our own extreme actions, we too must be mindful and responsible. We must accept the challenge of achieving and maintaining balanced awareness. If we fail to do so, we may find ourselves playing the role of the terrorist rather than the hero. Of course, similar lofty ambitions to Ming-Dao's Scholar Warrior, also come out of other cultural traditions: the Greek notion of the Philosopher-King, the Jeffersonian image of a Farmer-Politician, the American Indian ambition of the Medicine Man Warrior, and so forth.

"Acceptable extremism" is certainly possible, but the criteria are far more demanding than most of us can imagine. Narrow extremism (or myopic fanaticism), on the other hand, while commonplace in contemporary society, might be the most dangerous tendency of our times.

~

PART TWO

REENGINEERING WASTEFUL SYSTEMS

Part I considered psychological factors (e.g., desire to maximize consumption, focus upon short-term gains and losses, desire for large families) that make humans (in the aggregate) burdensome for the earth and its ecosystems. Suggestions for curbing our desires for excess in these domains were provided in part I. Part III will foster these initiatives toward voluntary simplicity by humans, by highlighting the strands of philosophies of the good life that are found in our moral traditions. Lives of excessive individual consumption, materialism, and the focus on individual welfare (as opposed to concern for the good of the community) are anathema to virtually all religious belief systems.

However, there lies an array of important social mechanisms that stand between the negative psychological tendencies traced in part I and the morally generated, environmentally appropriate philosophies of the good life still to be elaborated in part III. These mechanisms are the social realities of the societies that are responsible for the contemporary lifestyles that currently endanger our earth and its ecosystems. Generally speaking, in Third World countries, the systems that encourage people to have large families are particularly problematic. On the other hand, for First World countries, the systems that foster overconsumption are most problematic. Part II demonstrates some mechanisms (e.g., taxation policies, technological improvements) that might prove useful in working toward our sustainable life goals.

Chapters 6 and 7 deal with individual-level decisions about saving money and spending it. Money is the topic, first, because it enables us to *prove* so concretely the important points of humans' tendencies to overconsume in the present rather than investing in better futures for ourselves and succeeding generations. Second, your best training for a life of voluntary simplicity comes from gaining self-control via mastery of one's own personal finances. The axiom "Physician, heal thyself" (before you try to heal others) represents sage advice. Similarly, you should master your own investing and consuming habits before you attempt to tell others—and society as well—how to conduct their business. View chapters 6 and 7 as basic training in the ways of responsible living that are currently in short supply at the dawn of the newest century.

Chapter 8 describes green taxes in detail. Green taxes represent the improvement to our form of free market capitalism that will change the economic system from its current status as the preeminent producer of waste and environmental destruction, to its future role as the conduit for developing the proenvironmental lifestyles (and technological systems) of the twenty-first century. It is virtually impossible (in my opinion) to overestimate the importance of green taxes in solving environmental problems—if we only possess the political will to use them.

Chapter 9 also looks at systems that will help all of us be more responsible caretakers of our earth. However, this chapter focuses upon three examples of the roles that dreams (or hopeful stories of the future) play in actually creating better futures for all of us.

CHAPTER SIX

~

Habits at First Are Silken Threads

This chapter considers small differences in college graduates' habits in saving money. We will see that, in time, silken saving habits can produce cable-like forces that strangle otherwise "successful" careers and lives. Entertain a thought experiment about four successful Notre Dame graduates (two married couples). The force of this exercise will come from its fidelity to the actual financial facts of recent Notre Dame graduates' experience (circa, 1990). The lesson is that small, silken differences in savings habits can, over time, create levels of debt that seriously diminish the quality of our lives.

A Thought Experiment

Imagine two sets of identical twins (one set of males [Adam and Bob], one set of females [Alicia and Barbara]) who decided to marry one another (Adam marries Alicia: Couple A; Bob marries Barbara: Couple B) upon graduating from Notre Dame. My reason for imagining pairs of identical twins who marry is that I want to make these pairs equal in every way (e.g., intellectual prowess, motivation and work habits, investment acumen) save one—Couple A likes to spend 95 percent of their after-tax income, while Couple B chooses to spend 85 percent of their after-tax income. That one small difference between the pairs of imaginary couples will be responsible for all their differences in assets at retirement. The habit of spending 85 percent versus 95 percent of income represents a fragile thread that, over a 43-year working career, can create a debt cage.

A few realistic starting values and constants must be determined before we can begin our thought experiment. In my "Psychology of Everyday Life" course I note that Notre Dame Arts and Letters graduates average $26,000 for their starting salaries. If both spouses work, the couple would earn $52,000 per year before taxes. The IRS estimates that such a couple would pay approximately 23 percent for federal, state, local, and Social Security taxes. This estimate is too low if the wage earners are self-employed, and for the couples' later working years, when their incomes are much higher. However, the 23 percent tax bite will be considered constant throughout each couple's working career.

Notre Dame's office of financial aid says that the average level of student loan indebtedness of graduates is now $16,250—or $32,500 for each couple. Students also tend to have about $3,750 ($7,500 per couple) in other debts (e.g., credit card debt, personal loans, auto loans). Thus, the starting value for salaries (after taxes) for Couples A and B in table 6.1 is $40,000, and the couples' assets are entered for both as a $40,000 debt. The interest rates on student loans range from 5 percent to 7.4 percent; auto loans are currently around 9 percent; while my colleagues' credit cards charge from 16 percent to 21 percent annually on unpaid balances. An overall interest rate of 10 percent was chosen for this exercise.

My retirement money has averaged 7.15 percent (TIAA: bonds) and 14.06 percent (CREF: stocks) in annual returns for the last ten years—thus a 10 percent return on investment seems reasonable. If one chooses different starting values and constants, the net wealth of each couple at retirement will change. Later in this chapter other models will be run where different starting values and constants are used, in order to see the results of different scenarios. But since starting values and constants are the same for both the thrifty (B) and spendthrift (A) couples, the *difference* between the assets in table 6.1 of Couples A and B at retirement represents the cable-like vice that develops from the fragile thread of a savings habit that persists over 43 years.

Table 6.1 reveals that Couple A (5 percent savings rate) must immediately declare personal bankruptcy if they retire at age 65, since they are $325,987 in debt and they no longer have salaries that justify carrying such a high level of personal indebtedness. Couple B (15 percent savings rate) retires with a positive net worth of $3,841,246. Since all factors (including professional success as measured by annual salary) were equal for both couples, the enormous differences in terminal outcomes (bankruptcy

Table 6.1. Differences over time in assets for a couple who saves 5 percent of their after-tax income (Couple A) versus a couple that saves 15 percent of their after-tax income (Couple B)

	Salaries of A and B	Assets A	Couple A Interest Expense A (yr)	Savings A(yr)	Assets B	Couple B Interest Expense B (yr)	Savings B (yr)
Start	40,000	-40,000			-40,000		
End yr 1	42,000	-42,000	4,000	2,000	-38,000	4,000	6,000
End yr 2	44,100	-44,100	4,200	2,100	-35,500	3,800	6,300
End yr 3	46,305	-46,305	4,410	2,205	-32,435	3,550	6,615
End yr 4	48,620	-48,620	4,631	2,315	-28,733	3,244	6,946
End yr 5	51,051	-51,052	4,862	2,431	-24,313	2,873	7,293
End yr 10	65,156	-65,156	6,205	3,103	12,032	(248)	9,308
End yr 15	83,157	-83,157	7,920	3,960	84,708	(6,621)	11,880
End yr 20	106,132	-106,132	10,108	5,054	219,804	(18,604)	15,162
End yr 25	135,454	-135,454	12,900	6,450	460,414	(40,097)	19,351
End yr 30	172,878	-172,878	16,465	8,232	877,319	(77,511)	24,697
End yr 35	220,641	-220,641	21,013	10,507	1,586,273	(141,341)	31,820
End yr 40	281,600	-281,600	26,819	13,410	2,775,942	(248,701)	40,229
End yr 43 (Age 65)	325,987	-325,987	31,046	15,523	3,841,246	(344,971)	46,570
		$32,598 in interest expenses due every year of retirement without reducing total indebtedness			$384,124 of interest is available every year of retirement without touching principle		

( ) in Interest Expense reflects a positive return on investment. Also, all returns on investments are treated as tax deferred, since 15 percent of earnings can be tax sheltered each year under combinations of company retirement plans, SEPs, Keoghs, and IRAs.

versus wealth) are due *solely* to the couples' different saving habits (i.e., 5 percent versus 15 percent).

Out of the Depths of Debt I Cry unto Thee

I'm old enough to remember the days when virtually everyone graduated from college debt-free. Those of us who couldn't afford the price of full-time college simply worked during the day and attended night school. Or we might, instead, take a year off to earn money to continue our college education. We (and our parents also) held an old-fashioned belief—that money ought to be earned before it is spent. To dramatize how our current romance with debt serves to imprison our futures, run a model that simply changes the starting value of each couple's assets from minus $40,000 to 0. Will this change result in a $40,000 gain to each couple's retirement bottom line? Hardly! Couple A's assets at retirement will now be $2,083,616 instead of being $325,987 in debt. The $40,000 debt at graduation cost Couple A

$2,409,603 over the 43 years of this exercise. Couple B now retires with assets of $6,250,848 instead of $3,841,246. The analysis presented in table 6.1 highlights a personal characteristic (namely, the couples' savings habits) as the critical cause of Couple A's difficulty. Conversely, this last model suggests that debt might be the root of the problem. By examining the results of several models one begins to recognize the many variables involved in financial success or failure.

I believe that the finest graduation gift a parent might give would be to retire a portion of a graduate's indebtedness. How can Notre Dame work toward lessening the crushing debt load that threatens to diminish our graduates' futures? Providing more scholarship assistance is an obvious answer. As a member of Notre Dame's Faculty Board on Athletics, I have witnessed contributions by the athletic department of more than $25 million over the last four years into the university's unrestricted scholarships fund. By such enlightened policies, the university strives to lower graduates' crushing burden of debt.

What can friends of the university do in this regard? Contribute to unrestricted scholarships in the next annual fund drive. Unfortunately, scholarship endowment was the single category that was most seriously underfunded in Notre Dame's Strategic Moment campaign. Or imagine the power that a handful of fellowships that removed graduates' indebtedness would possess, if these awards were given to graduating seniors who committed to low-paying jobs that honored Notre Dame's Catholic social values.

Finally, what can I do to fight the demon of debt and the crippling habit of profligate spending? Like most educators, I can fairly claim "Gold and silver I have little. . . ." However, I do have access to the minds and hearts of many soon-to-be-Notre Dame graduates. Perhaps by helping students in my courses to spin the fragile threads of habits of thrift, I can help to avert the tragedies represented in table 6.1 by Couple A.

In Praise of Foresight

Mark Twain once quipped, "I've seen many tragedies in my life: Fortunately most of them never occurred." As always, Twain revealed deep insights into the workings of human nature at which psychologists can only marvel. Foresight represents a person's finest defense against life's tragedies. Recall that Karl Popper highlighted the power of imaginative foresight by claiming that humans are lucky—they can die hundreds of times in their imagination, rather than once in reality. I have gone broke hundreds of times in my imagination. Each time this tragedy occurs, I become a little clearer about exactly what I need to do to lessen the chances of this tragedy occurring in reality.

Glasses are prosthetic devices that improve our sight; artificial knees and hips aid impaired mobility. Is there any prosthetic device that might improve one's imaginative foresight? One unlikely candidate is the computer.

Some students fight off the implications of the data in table 6.1 by challenging the assumptions and starting values buried in the model that produces such startling and troubling conclusions. For example, some science, business, or engineering majors will undoubtedly note that their average starting salaries will be considerably higher than the $52,000 that a couple of arts and letters majors might expect. Computers allow us to fast-forward to this very different possible future in seconds with a few quick keyboard strokes. We simply change the salaries starting value from $40,000 to $51,000 (i.e., $33,000 x 2 people = $66,000 minus 23 percent for taxes = $51,000).

Surely, students think, $66,000 per year of income will overcome $40,000 in debt, even if the couple is a spendthrift pair who save only 5 percent of their after-tax income. Leaving all factors (save salaries) in table 6.1 unchanged and rerunning the model reveals that Couple B's retirement nest egg grows from $3,841,246 to $5,560,229. While Couple A now does not have to declare bankruptcy upon retiring, their nest egg is a paltry $247,008—less than half a year's worth of their salaries at the time they retired. It seems that even substantial starting salaries (and 5 percent yearly raises) are unable to offset the effects of debt and profligate spending habits. These surprising findings validate Logan Smith's observation that "Solvency is entirely a matter of temperament and not of income." Do you know the current average saving rate of American families? I'm sad to say it's a paltry 1 percent!

Finally, readers might mistakenly conclude that a couple's problems are over if they simply save 15 percent of after-tax salaries. If, for example, a middle-income couple has a large initial debt (like $60,000 or $70,000) and if their investments were to average only 4 percent to 5 percent per year return, then their assets would be insufficient to meet their retirement needs. Thus, good savings habits, while extremely important, do not guarantee savings success. Progress toward debt repayment and securing ample retirement funds must constantly be monitored to foresee the impacts of any changes in salary, interest rates on debt, inflation, rates of return on investments, and the like.

Growth: Arithmetic or Geometric?

In my course, students are given the starting values and constants that will yield the data in table 6.1. Their first homework assignment is to calculate the yearly values found in the table. Even with the aid of a calculator, it takes almost a day to calculate the values in table 6.1.

Values obtained for approximately the first ten years generally conform to students' expectations of how savings and debt grow. But eventually the calculated levels of wealth and debt begin to shock these undergraduates. Why is it that so many people are shocked by the enormous wealth and debt that one can accumulate over time? Lend me a paragraph or two of your time and attention to milk your intuition regarding how we often misunderstand growth rates.

Please answer *each* of the three questions separately below *before* reading any further. Which of the following choices would you take in each case?

A. A penny that doubled tax deferred every day for a week, or one million dollars?

B. A penny that doubled tax deferred every day for a month, or one million dollars?

C. A penny that doubled tax deferred every day for a year, or one million dollars?

Few people take the doubling penny for a week—as seven time blocks is clearly a short-term proposition. In fact, the doubling penny is worth only $1.28 after seven doubles. Conversely, intuition usually suggests that a penny that doubles 365 times (question C) would be quite valuable indeed. It is question B (an investment that compounds 31 times) that seems to produce a split in college students' intuitions (about half take the doubling penny, the other half take the million dollars). At the end of the second week the compounding penny rises in value from $1.28 to $163.84. At the end of the third week the penny is worth $21,611.52, and it grows to $2,782,418.56 by the end of week 4. So the doubling penny wins after four weeks. But the typical month is slightly longer than four weeks—it's 31 days. Why quibble over a paltry three more compoundings? Because it makes almost a *20-million-dollar* difference ($22,259,344.48 versus $2,782,418.56)!

What is wrong with our intuition when many of us select $1,000,000 instead of the $2,782,418 option (the penny that doubles every day for four weeks)? Psychologically speaking, we mistakenly think we are dealing with an *arithmetic* progression when, in fact, untaxed, compound interest (and debt also) grows *geometrically*. How can our intuitions be deceived so badly?

Figure 6.1 might be the most important geometric function one will ever study. The solid line does *not* depict a theoretical function, it plots the exact figures of the human population of our world over time (it is the

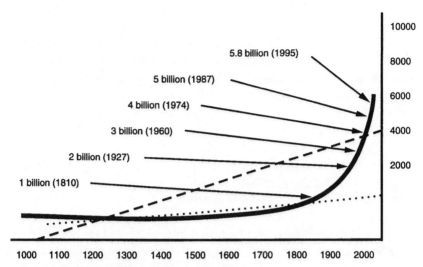

Figure 6.1. World population 1000 A.D. to 1995 A.D.
Source: Population Reference Bureau (1989).

same data as presented in table 6.1). The dotted line is the theoretical function that depicts the data from year 1000 A.D. to year 1800 A.D.—as if these data were the result of an arithmetic function. Early in a geometric function one can easily mistake it for an arithmetic function, as the predictions do not differ greatly from one another. Humans tend to focus almost solely upon short-term impacts, so assuming linearity (or an arithmetic function) still provides pretty good approximations *in the short run* (even though this assumption is incorrect). The dashed line is the line of best fit (again assuming linearity) for the data from 1000 A.D. to 1995 A.D. The expected global population in the year 2000 (assuming linearity) would be about 4 billion people. Given that the earth's population went over to 6 billion in 1999, that prediction is already shown to be wrong. Conversely, assuming that population grows geometrically, the data in figure 6.1 (from 1000 A.D. to 1995 A.D.) suggest that the planet's population in 2000 A.D. will be about 6.1 billion people. The geometric prediction will undoubtedly prove to be more accurate than the prediction that assumes an arithmetic function. The point is that over time the predictions of geometric functions differ dramatically from predictions that assume linearity. Thus, late in the games of compounding debt, untaxed compounding interest, global population, and the like, people are likely to be stunned at how quickly the numbers at stake will increase.

Education for Life

You may not have noticed, but this chapter is concerned with building character. It deals with acts of saving and spending, habits of thrift and profligacy, character traits like self-reliance and dependency, and destinies that are financially satisfying or tragic. Rather than being haphazardly related to one another, Charles Reade claims these four domains of human experience are, in fact, hierarchically related:

Sow an act, and you reap a habit.
Sow a habit, and you reap your character.
Sow your character, and you reap a destiny.

The implication of this ordering is that humans should focus upon doing the little things correctly—acts produce habits that build the character that determines one's destiny. A satisfying destiny in life often represents the natural outgrowth of thousands of well-chosen acts.

Education should not remain theoretical and abstract—it should be useful. Education also should help us to lead better lives. For years I have taught students that people overemphasize short-term pleasures and pain relative to any action's long-term consequences in their decision-making calculus. However, I'm afraid such theoretical statements were often far too abstract to exert real impact upon my students' lives. Of late, I have tried to spend more time helping students to trace both the short- and long-term consequences of many actions in their daily lives. Here the computer is rapidly becoming an invaluable resource, and this is not simply true for issues of personal finance. *Sim Earth* is a program that enables students to make choices regarding world population growth in the future, levels of economic activity, amount of investment in ecologically appropriate technologies, etc. The computer then demonstrates the ways in which our world will change in the future based upon the specific choices the student makes. This complex elaboration of long-term ecological consequences is similar to showing the long-term differences in assets at retirement if one were to select a 5 percent savings rate rather than a 15 percent savings rate. Similarly, *Sim City 2000* enables young public policy analysts to build different constellations of infrastructure (e.g., roads, power plants, schools, libraries) for an imaginary city. The program then spins-out a plausible future that favors domains that received investment versus those that are left neglected. My "Psychology of Everyday Life" course also deals with important issues like building and maintaining marital relationships, childrearing strategies, substance abuse, and many more. I am unaware of any *Sim Earth-* or *Sim City 2000*-type computer programs that demonstrate the long-term effects of attention paid to spouses, children, good health, etc. However, I am confident that such aids to our imaginative foresight in these domains will soon become available.

A sound education ought to closely examine the fragile threads of students' habits (such as saving, spending, reading to one's children, serious discussions with a spouse, exercise, etc.) that over time will mold students' characters and create their destinies. For what does it profit our students if they learn about the whole world, but lose control of their own lives?

CHAPTER SEVEN

~

Cheap Is Beautiful: Is Your Money Working as Hard as You Are?

Perhaps my natural frugality comes from my parents' incessant use of maxims such as "Willful waste makes woeful want," or the simpler "Waste not—want not." Or perhaps it was their frequent reminders that "A penny saved is a penny earned." [Actually, a penny saved is equal to about 1.48 pennies earned, if one is in the 31 percent federal tax bracket, allowing for 14 percent Social Security taxes, a 3 percent state tax rate, and no county or city taxes— as is the case in South Bend, Indiana]. See what I mean? I'm engrossed with the real, total cost of the things we purchase and consume. It is quite possible that my fixation is due to parental training—or perhaps I was just born to be cheap.

I am amazed at how economically shortsighted are the actions of many intelligent people. For example, most people today are under great economic pressure. Since we all would like to be responsible in our personal finances, my neighbors, students, and friends who find themselves in an economic mess, invariably reach for the same solution—*they try to earn more money*. While the impulse might be laudable, I'd like to criticize the wisdom of this strategy. My first objection to the "earning one's way out of debt" strategy is simple. As shown above, it can require $1,480 in additional earnings to achieve the same effect as a $1,000 reduction in spending. [Actually, for me to buy a $1,000 wristwatch would require $1,554 in additional earnings. This is because, in South Bend, we pay a 5 percent sales tax, and one must also pay federal, state, and Social Security taxes on the sales tax that we are routinely charged. This wasn't always the case, as we were able to deduct sales taxes paid on our federal tax return until that rule was changed in the 1980s. But I digress—or do I?]

Rule #1: Spending cuts are far more effective than increased earnings in escaping a household financial crisis. But this fact does not represent my primary reason for bashing the "earn your way out of economic difficulties" strategy. I see terrible, unintended consequences on personal, family, and work productivity and happiness when my neighbors take on a second job; when faculty colleagues do more private consulting; when my students get part-time jobs; and so forth. In a real sense, we diminish our lives whenever we overwork. Unfortunately, too many of us are already working too hard—and still, we are experiencing financial difficulties. An author of a recent book interviewed dozens of dying people and asked how they would live their lives differently, if they were given the chance. *None* said that they would spend more time at work.

As a psychologist, I'm compelled to ask why so many of us are overworking ourselves into early graves, when there often is a more effective solution readily available to ease financial strains? Why don't we recognize the enormous power of spending less, consuming less, and of generally appreciating the beauty of frugality? My opponent in this essay is the cumulative effect of many hundreds of billions—perhaps trillions—of dollars of advertising propaganda that have been hurled at each of us over the years. My tasks are (1) to plead with you to seriously reconsider what items in your lives are luxuries rather than necessities, and (2) to show how we might obtain these necessities and luxuries in ways that greatly reduce the amount we spend for them.

I offer these suggestions to help relieve the psychological strain many experience due to financial difficulties. We might thereby avoid the consequences of overwork that result from our efforts to earn our way out of financial messes. As examples, I'll consider the purchase of a range of goods and services—light, diamonds, heat, wristwatches, tuna fish, a housekeeper, and automobiles. I'd love to consider life insurance, but the industry has made that commodity so complex that the analysis would surely exhaust your patience. Finally, thoughts of "cutting back" and "reducing one's standard of living" generally bring about a tightening of the stomach and jaw muscles. Please put away your grim countenance, as what I am about to show you is absolutely fascinating.

Are you now under stress due to a lack of money? People with incomes ranging from $5,000 to $500,000 answer "yes" to such queries. But that raises a puzzling question. How can people who earn 100 *times* more than what others earn still have the same problem? The puzzle's solution lies in a reality that comes close to being a universal law of human nature. That is, unless one consciously struggles against the tendency to overspend, one's "necessary expenses" will always grow to equal one's income. So let's first carefully examine some "necessary expenses."

Necessities or Luxuries?

Consider light, a car, a wristwatch, tuna fish, diamonds, heat, and a housekeeper. With the exception of diamonds, I can make a case that all represent necessities for certain people. But the important issue is, are they necessities or luxuries for me and for you? For me, light, a car, tuna fish (or some nutritious food to replace it), and heat might be seen as necessities—the rest are luxuries. One's circumstances determine what constitutes a luxury. For example, for some of my friends in Manhattan, automobiles are not a necessity. However, in South Bend, cars are close to necessary. Since virtually every adult owns a wristwatch, have I erred in calling it a luxury? Not at all. I've never owned a wristwatch, and I can't remember the last time I missed having one. The important point is that something is not a necessity simply because you've always owned one (e.g., a car), or because everyone you know owns one (e.g., a wristwatch). If your life would be significantly diminished by not spending money on an item or service, then it can reasonably be considered a necessity for you. Luxuries are fair game for spending cuts, but unless your financial circumstances are truly desperate, one should not consider forgoing a necessity.

By now, the cynical reader has me pegged as one of those lifeless, grinch-types who wants to suck all the pleasure out of life by making people forgo the luxuries that bring joy to life. Rather, I'm trying to show ways that enable you to afford even more pleasurable luxuries in your life. What follows is a strategy for maximizing (in the long run) the luxuries that you enjoy. In fact, if you are in the early part of your earning career, and if you can now afford to save 10 percent of your income (using George Clason's 1923 rule of thumb), then no spending cuts are necessary. If you are farther along in your earning career—and are still just making ends meet—a greater than 10 percent surplus will be required.

To What Uses Might Money Saved from Earnings and Spending Cuts Be Put?

What follows is a rank-ordering of good uses for your savings.

1. Pay off debts. When someone turns over his or her personal finances to a pro, this is one of the pro's first moves. Credit card debt gets paid first, prepayment of a home mortgage occurs last.
2. Invest savings where doing so results in income reduction for tax purposes (e.g., SEPs, Keoghs, company retirement plans) and/or tax deferred (or exempt) earnings growth (e.g., IRAs—especially Roth IRAs!)
3. Invest in technologies that produce their own spending reductions. More on this strategy later under "Necessity: Where Is The Sting?"
4. Make other investments that result in no particular spending reductions or tax advantage (e.g., stocks, bonds). The importance of this suggestion will increase in the future because capital gains tax rates are now on the decline.

The older I get, the more I realize that wisdom is cloaked in simplicity—not complexity. Consider the four suggested ways to use our savings. Why does debt reduction come first? Because interest on our debt represents an expense for which we have nothing to show. Spend money on tuna and you've got something to eat—even with diamonds you at least have something attractive to wear or sell later. The simple wisdom behind the second investment suggestion—tax-favored investments—can be garnered from the following quick exercise.

Forgoing Short-Term Pleasures for Long-Term Riches

In the example of the penny that doubles each day, recall that the penny had grown to $2,782,418.56 by the end of week 4. So the doubling penny wins after four weeks. But the typical month is slightly longer than four weeks—it's 31 days. Why quibble over a paltry three more compoundings? Because it makes almost a *20-million-dollar* difference ($22,259,344.48 versus $2,782,418.56)!

Thirty-one *tax-deferred* compoundings is an interesting figure because if you started working (and saving for your retirement) at age 25, your nest egg would have compounded 31 times by age 56. [Of course, our doubling penny example involved two important simplification strategies. Your total contribution to this retirement plan is $.01 (which is ridiculously low) and your annual rate of return is 100 percent (which is ridiculously high).] A more realistic example of the miracle of untaxed, compound interest would be if you invested $2,000 in your IRA account at age 25 and received an 8 percent return (the current yield on U.S. Treasury Bonds as I wrote this chapter). That initial $2,000 alone will have grown to $32,000 if you retired at age 61. When that figure is added to the yields from other $2,000 contributions made at ages 26, 27, 28, . . . , 61 you're soon talking about a nice nest egg (approximately $612,000).

Did I say earlier that a 100 percent per year rate of return is ridiculously high? In showing the simple wisdom in suggestion #3 above (i.e., investments that result in future spending reductions), we'll find that a 100 percent return isn't ridiculous at all.

Necessity: Where Is Thy Sting?
Let's quickly review where we are. For a lucky few, your earnings exceed all your expenses by 10 percent or more—simply invest this surplus in some mix of the four investment strategies above. For many other readers, a number of expenses will have to be identified as luxuries, and cut back until income exceeds total expenses by at least the 10 percent per year to be invested. For each of us, surprise items (like a wristwatch) can be added to the usual list of luxury suspects (e.g., movies, vacations, diamonds, lottery tickets, etc.). However, let's consider a more difficult case. For a few readers, even after their luxury expenses have been reasonably purged, their income still might not exceed their expenses for necessities by 10 percent. The key here is to take whatever money you have (no matter how small) and use it to purchase necessities in a way that will cut future expenses.

A story is told that someone asked the economist John Kenneth Galbraith what was the best investment he could imagine. If the questioner had stocks like Thunderbolt Technologies and Wildcat Oil in mind, he or she must surely be shocked when Galbraith reportedly advised that the next time tuna fish went on sale, he or she was to buy several cans and put it under the bed until it was needed next. Let's carefully examine the wisdom in Galbraith's investment strategy. First, we must be dealing with a *necessity*. We know that tomorrow, next week, and next month we'll need tuna fish (or some other nutritious food). Second, the commodity purchased must be nonperishable (buying a hundred loaves of bread that soon mold is ill-advised). Third, at my supermarket, tuna normally sells for $.59 for a 5½ oz. can, but periodically goes on sale for $.39. My family consumes about 5 cans of tuna each week. Thus, if I buy 10 cans of tuna on sale, I will save $2.00 in spending over the next two weeks [10 cans at $.59 = $5.90 minus $3.90

(sale cost) = $2.00 savings]. A $2.00 savings on a $3.90 investment yields over 50 percent return on investment over a two-week period. One's annualized rate of return would be over 2,600 percent by repeatedly employing this investment strategy. Galbraith is a genius! Further, anyone can come up with $3.90 to begin cutting his or her future expenses. But there are problems on the horizon for this simple strategy. One must take the $2.00 savings and immediately reinvest it to achieve other expense reductions. [Buy two lottery tickets and you've wasted Galbraith's wisdom.] But there are limits to how much tuna one ought to consume—and it seems that tuna rarely goes on sale just when we need it. Fortunately, savings from wise food investments can be used to lower the future costs of other necessities.

What will you do the next time a 100-watt incandescent light bulb burns out in your kitchen? Try investing your "tuna savings" in a GE 28-watt compact fluorescent light bulb (that sells for $20) that gives comparable light to a 100-watt incandescent bulb (that sells for $.75). "What?" you rage. "Throw away my hard-earned 'tuna money' by overpaying for some high-tech light bulb? I thought you said *cheap* is beautiful!" But by now you realize that we're not talking about being "cheap" in this chapter—we're discussing being thrifty, frugal, and financially wise.

Consumers typically look for "bargains," which often turn out to be unwise investments. Investors, on the other hand, are not focused solely upon prices—they consider the likely rates of return on their investments. Let's examine the total cost of that 28-watt compact fluorescent bulb versus the $.75 bargain. First, the compact fluorescent bulb lasts for 10,000 hours versus 750 hours for the 100-watt incandescent—so you'll need to purchase more than 13 incandescent bulbs before the compact fluorescent bulb burns out. Thus, the materials costs are $20 for the compact fluorescent bulb versus $9.75 (13 x $.75) for the incandescents. But what of the electricity costs? If your electricity sells for $.08/kilowatt hour (the national average) the compact fluorescent consumes $22.40 in electricity over 10,000 hours; the incandescent bulbs consume $80 in electricity. Thus, by wisely investing $20 in a high-tech lighting appliance, you save $47.35 [($9.75 + $80) − ($20 + $22.40) = $47.35].

If your kitchen light is on for less than seven hours a day, your electricity savings are realized over two years for an annualized rate of return of over 115 percent per annum. I install a few more compact fluorescent bulbs in my home whenever I have a little extra cash from "tuna money," "cranberry juice money," "toilet paper money," etc. I now have about forty of these lighting money-savers working hard to cut my monthly electricity bill. I've also reduced my heating and air conditioning costs dramatically by installing a geothermal heating and cooling unit, when my gas furnace conked out about eight years ago. The additional cost of the geothermal unit ($2,400 minus a utility company rebate and property tax refunds) is now completely recovered, and the geothermal unit saves about $100 per month in natural gas charges in the winter, and about $50 per month in electricity charges in the summer. Money invested in reducing energy consumption also has the positive effect of helping the ecology of our planet, but for the present we'll focus solely upon the economic benefits of energy-efficient technologies.

As a final thought on strategy #3, techniques for reducing the costs of necessities, let me tell you that I have not yet paid $10,000 or more for an automobile, even though we purchase full-size cars because we routinely take many of my children's friends to athletic games and practices. Here's how we do it—we buy used cars from rental companies, rather than autos from used car lots. The value of an automobile declines precipitously in its first year of use. The trick is to get a good automobile (rather than picking up someone else's "lemon") after that steep decline in value has occurred. Car rental companies (e.g., Hertz, Avis, National) hold their stock until preset limits are hit (e.g., one year, 30,000 miles). Or if new stock arrives, some autos are sold before the limits are reached. My last four cars averaged eight months and 22,000 miles of use. Equivalent new autos still on sale (my purchases occurred near the end of the model year) listed for about $8,000 more than the price that I paid. Since rental car companies must turn over all of their stock within a brief time period, the base rate of "lemons" that rental companies sell should be about equal to the base rate for new cars—likely a smaller rate of "lemons" than one might find among year-old cars on a used car lot.

In keeping with suggestion #1 to pay off debts immediately, I try to stay with my old car until I have saved enough cash to pay for a "new" car (thus never paying auto loan finance charges). I was able to pay cash for my geothermal unit because one of my used rental auto purchases cost far less than I had expected. My phantom monthly "car payments," "electricity bill savings," and "natural gas savings" are now used to make prepayments on my home mortgage principal. These additional payments are simply added to the base mortgage payments suggested by our bank each month. Of course, it has taken twenty years of spending frugality to achieve the positive cash flow that now allows mortgage prepayments. We might have reached that point sooner had we not chosen over the years to purchase certain luxuries. We have always paid top-dollar for childcare and education, we take frequent, short vacations, we receive help with our housework once a week, we make regular charitable contributions, and we contribute to the support of several of our relatives. We were not in a position to enjoy any of these luxuries twenty years ago. However, we trust we will be able to enjoy many more luxuries twenty years from now.

A Psychology for the Twenty-First Century

For centuries, blackness had been seared into our psyches as something ugly, sinister, and loathsome. The black movement of the 1960s began a reprogramming of our collective consciousness with the slogan "Black is beautiful!" A similar rethinking of the foundations of economic theory, given the ecological realities of the twenty-first century, was begun by the British economist E. F. Schumacher under the title *Small Is Beautiful*. Current work, against the beliefs that growth and increased consumption represent economic values, has been offered by Garrett Hardin (1993; *Living Within Limits*) and Alan Durning (1992; *How Much Is Enough?*). We now understand that *sustainable* growth and development (rather than unlimited growth) represent the "goods" (i.e., values) to be desired, given the realities of the twenty-first century's overcrowded world. For too long our thinking has been trapped by the assumptions of "cowboy economics" (see Boulding 1966)— the belief that growth, development, and consumption could go on forever. If something represented a "good" (such as the GDP, the size of a country's population, the amount of luxuries one consumed, etc.), then it followed (from cowboy economics) that more was necessarily better.

The psychology and economics of the twenty-first century will value a *sustainable balancing* of relative goods in our life-choices. Thus, while the consumption of certain quantities of necessities is inevitable, the overconsumption of necessities and luxuries is to be discouraged. Thrift, frugality, and the ability to delay gratification will be cardinal virtues of our psychologies and economics of the future. However, to understand the forces against which these new ways of thinking now struggle, we will consider how advertising strives to convince us that a diamond ring is a necessity.

In a sense, diamond jewelry might be the ultimate luxury. Jewelry is certainly not necessary for life; one can obtain virtually indistinguishable jewelry (using zirconium) for a tiny fraction of the cost of diamond jewelry; and while raw diamonds might occasionally be a good investment, diamond jewelry almost never is. No one in our family has diamond jewelry! But rather than saying that last sentence proudly, I felt *guilty* in acknowledging that fact. Didn't my wife *deserve* a diamond engagement ring? Of course we had a case of graduate students' poverty when we married. But shouldn't I have made up for that oversight with a twentieth anniversary diamond pendant? If my choice to not purchase Nancy diamond jewelry simply reflects prudent fiscal management, why would I feel guilty? Pay special attention to the many advertisements for diamond jewelry that you encounter. "A diamond is forever!" (Am I less than fully committed to this relationship?); "Buy her a diamond ring, because she deserves the very best!" (Am I indirectly saying to Nancy that she's second-rate?); "A diamond anniversary pin to let her know you'd gladly do it all over again" (Am I having second thoughts about my wife?). Just because one is a psychologist doesn't mean he or she is immune to psychological persuasion. Am I being frugal? Or am I cheap, uncommitted, unappreciative, etc.? Is it in anyone's best interest for me to be conflicted about my choice to not purchase diamond jewelry?

Frontline did a PBS show on DeBeers—the worldwide diamond cartel—that showed how control over the diamond trade was maintained by incorporating into the cartel all new sources of diamonds that were discovered. Then DeBeers is faced with the problem of offsetting this additional supply by increasing the demand for diamonds. This is accomplished by means of a collusion between DeBeers and its retailers that leads to the advertisements quoted above. The Corporation for Public Broadcasting (1994, *The Diamond Empire*) provides a blatant example of how these co-conspirators strive to make what is clearly a luxury into a (psychological) necessity. DeBeers laid out its game plan to retailers whereby a marketing blitz would "make the twenty-fifth anniversary pendant *as obligatory as* the diamond engagement ring and the five-, ten-, and twenty-year gifts of diamond jewelry." Of course, DeBeers executives are reluctant to admit to us that they strive to persuade us that their luxury item is a necessity—they only communicate that reality to their business partners. Nevertheless, a lot of money has been spent (by DeBeers and others) to make me feel guilty about my decision *not* to buy their luxury commodities. Suppose I now decide to buy an anniversary diamond pendant for my wife. One might reasonably ask, "Who has control of my mind? Me or DeBeers?"

This chapter is not an antiluxury diatribe. Rather, it offers strategies for securing the financial ability to enjoy many luxuries over one's lifetime. To the extent that children today are taught to value immediate gratification at the expense of long-term financial health, it is an essay against this idol of our times. However, some psychologists believe the fight against such idols faces stiff competition. Recall Albee's insight,

> The capitalist system, in order to sell its plethora of manufactured goods, has had to enlist the help of the motivation researcher and the Madison Avenue ad agency to get rid of the excessive and ever growing pile of manufactured goods not really needed in our society. To encourage consumption in the absence of real need and to associate status and self-esteem with

wasteful consumption, it has been necessary to encourage relatively mind-less impulse buying and self-gratification. By now, we have raised several generations of people on endless and repetitive exhortations that it is all right to yield to impulse, to buy without guilt, and to consume without shame. Installment buying may have been the fatal blow to the self-denial of the Protestant ethic. (Albee 1977, 150)

None of the wisdom contained in this chapter represents an original in-sight of mine. For example, these ideas merely represent updates and elabo-rations of the first two (of seven) points for creating personal wealth articu-lated by George Clason in 1923, and represent insights originally formulated by Benjamin Franklin in the eighteenth century. [See Robbins (1989) for ex-plicit details on implementing Franklin's wisdom.]

Thoughts on the World's Largest Debtor
Lessons learned in the arena of personal finance may or may not be applica-ble for remedying the financial ills of a country. However, the parallels be-tween personal financial strategies and current governmental policy are strik-ing. Consideration of our government's current financial status suggests some form of fiscal reform is in order.

My parents' working careers spanned roughly the 40-year period from 1935 to 1975. My working career will cover roughly the 1975–2015 period. My children's peak earning years will likely begin in the second and third decades of the twenty-first century. What was the long-term financial condi-tion of our country, as my parents ceded responsibility to my generation for paying our country's shared bills in 1975? What will the nation's long-term financial health be like in 2015 when my children take over?

In 1975 the United States was a net creditor country—people and gov-ernments owed the United States more than our country owed to other peo-ple and governments. That is, our financial assets exceeded our debts. There-fore, for every dollar in taxes that my parents and I paid in 1975, my country could offer a dollar in services (e.g., national defense, welfare, farm subsidies, construction of infrastructure) without endangering the country's long-term financial health. We are now more than halfway through the 40-year inter-val of my generation's stewardship of our nation's financial health. It's time we faced up to our financial report card.

Our nation's financial assets are now exceeded by our debts by about $5 trillion (roughly the size of the national debt). Further, our budget deficit for 1994 was $200 billion—that is, our bills exceeded our income by that amount, and thus we slid that much further into debt. Our largest, single, yearly governmental expense now is *not* national defense, nor welfare, nor Medicare—it is the interest we pay on our national indebtedness (about $400 billion/year). For every tax dollar you and I now pay, 28 cents of it goes to service (i.e., to pay interest on) our government's debt. When the book is closed on my generation's stewardship of our nation's finances (in the year 2015) what percentage of our children's tax dollars will be required to service our national debt?

The report card for the country at the midpoint of my working life merits a clear failing grade. For the last twenty years we have been anemic earners (e.g., taxes paid) and profligate spenders (e.g., defense, entitlements, interest on debt) relative to other industrialized nations. Most of us have been unknowing participants in a terrible form of financial child abuse. Happily, I still have twenty more earning years to try to improve my final grade. Believe it or not, I am now urging my political representatives to raise our taxes slightly and to cut governmental spending dramatically. [In accord with the earlier finding that spending less is more effective than earning more.] Collectively we need to live more cheaply to ensure that our children are not overburdened by a crushing national debt. Sadly, the Bush administration just implemented huge, new tax cuts.

Get that grim look off your face, friend. One of the best-kept secrets of our age is that making sacrifices to earn a better future is one of the most satisfying activities that one can undertake. We have been so brainwashed by a culture of consumption and a creed of hedonism that we have forgotten the pleasures that naturally come from building, creating, sacrificing, and conserving (see Albee 1977). The challenge of developing fiscally responsible lifestyles is not a grim sentence to a lifetime of hard labor. Rather, being responsible to ourselves and our successors represents an intriguing challenge, the solution to which will be numbered among our lives' most important contributions. Leaving this world a better place than the world we inherited represents an exciting challenge. How we deal with such important challenges helps to give meaning and excitement to our lives. The winners of the game of life will not be the ones who have consumed the most (and run up the largest debts) when death comes calling—it will be those who gave more than they consumed. While most of us do not evaluate the success of our lives by our wealth, money is an important factor in how successful we are in achieving our lives' goals. This is because (as noted earlier), "If money be not thy servant, it will be thy master."

CHAPTER EIGHT

~

Green Taxes

Being responsive to the earth's ecological needs is often very frustrating for businesses. In the ecology literature, business and global overpopulation are routinely vilified as the primary causes of the many problems that threaten to compromise human life on our planet. However, research in ecological psychology reveals how businesses are sometimes victimized when they attempt to solve the ecological problems that they have been accused of having created. A brief example of how this can occur might prove illuminating.

GE's Problems in Bringing Good Things to Life

For all of its wonder, Thomas Edison's incandescent light bulb is tremendously *inefficient*. About 90 percent of the energy consumed produces heat rather than light. Compact fluorescent light bulbs give the same amount of light, using only 20 to 30 percent of the electricity that incandescent bulbs require. Shifting from incandescent to compact fluorescent bulbs would save consumers 70 to 80 percent of the lighting portion of their electricity bills. In addition, people who spend more money for air conditioning than they do for heat would also reap lower net energy bills, as the high heat levels produced by their incandescent bulbs would not have to be overcome by air conditioning.

Light-bulb efficiencies would *not* be an ecological issue if our electricity came from nonpolluting, renewable energy sources such as solar, tide, geothermal, or wind power. However, since nonrenewable, polluting energy sources (e.g., coal, oil, natural gas) supply the lion's share of the fuels that produce our electricity, light bulb inefficiencies are important ecological issues. Recognizing this fact, General Electric and other companies (e.g., Sylvania, Osram) have developed and aggressively marketed compact fluorescent bulbs. In spite of the fact that compact fluorescents are in the best economic interests of consumers (and the best ecological interests of our world), for the past fifteen years they have been a tough sell in the United States. Admittedly, earlier versions of the bulbs had several unattractive features that limited their appeal to consumers. However, present versions are greatly improved and are quite acceptable. Still, market penetration has been very limited. While I have more than forty compact fluorescent bulbs that are working hard to save money and electricity in my home, I've never seen more than two in anyone else's home. Have you seen significant numbers of compact fluorescents in anyone's home?

Most of the subjects in my research projects report that they have never heard of compact fluorescent bulbs. Yet, to its credit, GE is aggressively marketing them. I frequently see television ads for GE's compact fluorescent bulbs. [Have you seen the ad where a kid asks his friend Tommy, "How many grown-ups does it take to change a light bulb?" Reflecting upon the durability of compact fluorescents, Tommy wonders, "Why would anyone need to change a light bulb?"] Given GE's barrage of advertisement, it's strange that so many research subjects claim they have never heard of compact fluorescents. One wonders if people would buy them if they had heard of them.

In studies conducted at Notre Dame, we found that fewer than one in four people buy a compact fluorescent even after (a) learning of its ecological and economic benefits, (b) receiving a one-month free trial with the bulb, and (c) being offered a 20 percent price discount. If only one in four buys under those circumstances, how will we ever get substantial numbers of consumers to pay full price when they consider compact fluorescents on store shelves?

Shortsightedness—Thy Name Is Human!

As a child, I used to rush through every task—it was just part of my nature to do so. My father would stop me dead in my tracks as he chided me in his slow Southern drawl: "Slow down, boy. Life's a distance race, it's not a sprint." How right he was! The more one studies ecology, the more one learns that it is the long-term vision that is important. Short-term considerations are not nearly as important as they initially might seem. The more one studies psychology, the more one realizes that humans *almost always* sacrifice important long-term considerations to trivial short-term rewards or punishments. It's our credit card lifestyle: the live-for-today and don't-sweat-tomorrow mentality. When asked whether they'd prefer to receive $16 now or $20 a year from now, most Americans take the money and run. In doing so, they turn down a guaranteed, tax-free, 25 percent rate of return on their investment! Now how smart is that? Ornstein and Ehrlich (*New World, New Mind: Moving Toward Conscious Evolution*, 1989) argue convincingly that we have evolution to blame for our self-defeating preference for short-term thinking. Regardless of where this self-defeating, short-term outlook comes from, our challenge is to find ways to help direct people's actions toward producing good, long-term consequences.

The task for psychologists (and for GE and ecological activists) is to train people to prefer superior economic and ecological options over cheap, temporary need-satisfiers in the calculus of their decision making. Consider the following question as we begin to understand the lines of thinking that lead so many people to self-defeating choices. Is buying a light bulb more like buying a can of tuna fish or buying a share of stock?

If your gut reaction is that it was more like buying a can of tuna, then you are probably imagining yourself as a *consumer* in framing your choice between the incandescent or compact fluorescent bulbs. Consumers see themselves as having a "need"—for food, light, a car, etc.—that they try to satisfy at as low a cost as possible. If you need a can of tuna, you survey the range of prices for brands of tuna that are "good enough" for you, looking for one that might represent a "bargain." If purchasing a light bulb is similar (in your mind) to buying tuna, then that $.75 incandescent "bargain" will get you every time.

Conversely, when you buy stock you should not think like a consumer; you should think like an investor. Investors consider likely *rates of return* on their investments, and they also tend to think in longer time frames than do consumers. Using the figures calculated earlier, and assuming a light bulb is in use for 14 hours/day, the $20 investment in a compact fluorescent would yield $47.50 in savings in less than two years. That represents a guaranteed, tax-free, annual rate of return of almost 60 percent! Would any shrewd investor turn down that offer? Well, millions of us routinely do so.

The sad truth is that human shortsightedness maintains the needless waste of 70 percent to 80 percent of the electricity used for residential lighting today. GE and several other companies stand ready to sell us either highly efficient or very wasteful lighting devices. GE shareholders will be happy to know that the company's profit on one compact fluorescent is about the same as on ten incandescent bulbs. Thus, GE's fiduciary responsibility to its shareholders is satisfied whether or not customers choose the ecologically appropriate option. Yet, because we all care for the future of our planet, I believe that GE would be pleased if compact fluorescent sales dwarfed incandescent sales, instead of the current, opposite circumstance. Thus, in this case, American business is *not* the cause of this ecological difficulty. If any blame is to be assigned, it should be placed at the feet of shortsighted, consumer-oriented humans. We have met the enemy—and they are us!

It's as unfair to lump all ecological activists together as it is to lump all businesses together. Some environmental activists would not be pleased with me for placing blame with American consumers (and away from business) in the above example. But the theoretical divisions among ecologists go deeper still. For example, some (e.g., Glendinning 1995) see society as gripped by a social pathology called "techno-addiction." The road to societal recovery lies in rejecting our technology-dominated lives and slowly returning to a simpler way of life. From that perspective, a problem created by a relatively simple technology (such as an incandescent bulb) should *not* be cured by a more complex technological device (a compact fluorescent bulb), since more complex technologies move society even further in the wrong direction. Universal agreement about appropriate steps to solve environmental problems cannot be achieved—even among environmental activists. With that thought in mind, I'd like to present a general model that might be applied broadly to the many business-related causes of environmental deterioration. While not an infallible cure for environmental difficulties, the strategy can profitably be employed to lessen many environmental strains in a very business-friendly manner.

The Greening of the IRS

This cryptic heading suggests an answer to a riddle, "How can we initiate new taxes, but pay no more in taxes?" An answer might be by initiating "green taxes" that will replace dollar-for-dollar our federal income taxes. First, what is a green tax, and why is it a business-friendly way to environmental sanity?

Capitalizing upon your new knowledge of the finances of light bulbs, imagine that a green tax of $.10 was levied on the sale of all incandescent light bulbs (whether produced domestically or abroad). The cost is immediately passed on to the consumer, who now pays $.85 per bulb. Thus, GE's profit margin is unchanged. Consumers pay no more in total taxes because federal tax rates are lowered to produce income tax savings equal to the total of all green taxes collected. Thus, a consumption tax replaces an income tax dollar-for-dollar to produce no net change in taxation. As with sales taxes, business collects green taxes, which moves the IRS a bit further from our lives. Paul Hacken claims that if we took green taxes seriously, we might put the IRS completely out of business. Wouldn't that be a pleasant, indirect outcome!

The green tax on incandescent light bulbs would rise to $.20 in the second year, $.30 in the third year, and so on until the twentieth year, when the final green tax level of $2 per bulb would arrive. By then, we would almost all be converted to compact fluorescents because, at over $2.75 per bulb, who would prefer incandescents to compact fluorescents? Light-bulb companies continue to earn the same profit, but now it comes from the sale of efficient technologies rather than wasteful technologies. The twenty-year phase-in period enables all light-bulb companies the time to make whatever adjustments are necessary to adapt to the changing market conditions produced by the green tax.

Everyone knows that the income tax serves as a disincentive to earning, saving, and investing. If $10 billion were raised in green taxes on incandescent bulbs over a 20-year period, then $10 billion in disincentives would be removed from our income tax bills. However, there are known problems with all consumption taxes, and such problems will need to be worked out for any green taxes. But whereas other consumption taxes are crude—like saturation bombing—green taxes work with the precision of "smart" bombs. If we taxed *all* light bulbs (presumably because they are involved in producing pollution), the supply–demand laws suggest that people would buy fewer light bulbs—thereby cutting corporations' profits. With a green tax on incandescents, consumers will (in the longer run) spend a smaller percentage of their income on lighting, while corporate profits from light bulbs still go essentially unchanged.

Some industrial problems require an even finer-grained approach to green taxes. Instances where a good product–bad product distinction does not fit so easily require a more nuanced approach. For example, electric utilities use many energy sources to generate power (e.g., hydro, coal, natural gas, solar, oil). Rather than coarsely labeling some as "good" and others as "bad," a more precise tailoring of taxes would better serve our national interests. A panel of environmental experts might rank-order the various fuel sources with respect to many factors (e.g., amount and types of pollutants, domestically available–imported, renewable–nonrenewable), yielding the following relationships with respect to the undesirability of each fuel source:

Source Undesirability:

Coal = Oil > Natural gas > Hydro > Solar = Wind = Geothermal

Maximum green tax:

100% 100% 50% 25% 0% 0% 0%

The lower line indicates the percentage of some maximum level of green tax to be placed upon each energy source of electricity. Thus, the price of non-renewable, polluting, imported fuel sources would increase dramatically. Conversely, renewable, nonpolluting, domestic sources would pay no green tax. Again, such taxes might be phased in over twenty years, and the trillions of dollars raised would lead to enormous reductions in the federal income taxes we pay. The problem of ozone depletion (caused by chlorofluorocarbons) might have been solved via green taxes rather than the phased-in bans that were employed. Similarly, the ratio of fuel-efficient to fuel-inefficient cars on our highways could also be increased via green tax solutions.

Free Markets: Reality or Fiction?

Do green taxes represent unwelcome intrusions into the actions of our free marketplace? Perhaps to the surprise of many readers, my answer is "Absolutely not!" Many writers (e.g., Hardin 1993; Hawken 1993; Henderson 1981) have argued that our present markets are not free and properly functioning *precisely because not all* of the *real* costs of our goods and services are included in their market prices. Green taxes would allow us to enter real costs (e.g., the price of emitting greenhouse gases; producing acid rain; depleting nonrenewable resources; destroying natural habitats) into market prices. The destructive consequences of our business practices are currently being treated as externalities. Green taxes allow us to internalize these externalities, and thus would produce (perhaps for the first time) a complete, truly-free market that might then be able to work its wonders.

The renewable, efficient, and nonpolluting technologies that will dominate the twenty-first century cannot compete in a marketplace that will not fairly charge inefficient, polluting, nonrenewable competitors for their negative impacts. In the light-bulb example, because GE's sales and profits continue to come from their more wasteful, polluting product (i.e., incandescent bulbs), GE is virtually mandated not to move more aggressively in pushing the efficient technologies that we need to solve our ecological crises.

During the 1992 global environmental summit held in Rio de Janeiro, our Japanese and European competitors openly declared their belief that "the development of energy-efficient technologies represents the largest potential market in the history of the world." Because the prices of gasoline and electricity in Japan and Europe are far higher than they are in the United States (due to taxes that act like green taxes), American companies now possess a slight, short-term competitive edge. But these same American companies are crippled in their struggle to develop the technologies of efficiency *because* our energy costs are now artificially low. I fear that the long-term competitiveness of American business is now being sacrificed at the altar of a short-term competitive advantage.

Our low cost of energy also stimulates greater overall energy consumption. Is it any wonder that we, as Americans, are responsible for 26 percent of the world's energy consumption (United Nations 1998)—even though we have less than 10 percent of the world's population? Green taxes would be an excellent first step toward rectifying our overreliance on cheap energy. Such taxes would immediately make clean, renewable, energy-efficient, alternative technologies more cost-effective. The prospect of gradually increasing green taxes over the next two decades will enable American businesses to pursue the technologies of efficiency more aggressively, as we quickly phase-out the inefficient, polluting technologies of the twentieth century. Finally, as business collects more and more green tax revenues, we will approach that glorious day when we might say, "Remember the bad old days, when we used to have to pay income taxes. . . ."

CHAPTER NINE

~

Imagine!

Foresight (or the power to imagine possible futures) is one of the most important of all human skills (Howard 1993). This chapter traces three exercises in imagination (or foresight) that have important implications for the political, business, and economic systems that now dominate our lives. The first imaginative exercise will be easy for you to follow, since you are now familiar with green taxes.

A: What Will Happen If We Tax Gasoline Like Europeans Do?

The economist Hal Varian (who serves as the dean of the School of Information Management and Systems at the University of California at Berkeley) answered this section title's question in the October 19, 2000, edition of the *New York Times*.

First, it is a good idea to tax the consumption of goods that impose costs on other people. One person's consumption of gasoline increases emissions of carbon dioxide and other pollutants, and this imposes environmental costs on everyone. And even those who do not care much about the environment have to acknowledge that driving contributes to traffic congestion. Increased taxes on gasoline would reduce consumption, cutting both pollution and congestion.

But, you might argue, we already have taxes on gasoline: federal, state and local taxes average about 41 cents a gallon, or 28 percent of the price of gasoline. Isn't this enough? The problem is that the tax is used mostly to pay for road construction and maintenance. True, the gasoline tax decreases the use of gasoline, but the road subsidy increases its use.

If we subtract the subsidy from the tax, we end up with a net tax rate on gasoline in the United States of about 2 percent, which is much, much lower than net gasoline taxes in the rest of the world.

There is another, quite different reason to tax oil products.

Economists like to tax things that are in fixed supply because the same amount is available whether or not the tax is imposed. World oil supplies wax and wane in the short run depending on how effectively OPEC is enforcing production quotas. But in the long run, there is only so much oil. Taxing petroleum products will not reduce the total amount of oil in the ground, it will just slow the rate at which it is discovered and extracted.

Taxes on gasoline reduce the demand for oil, thereby reducing the price received by the suppliers of oil. And most of those suppliers are foreign: the United States now imports 56 percent of its oil, and OPEC countries control about three-fourths of the world's proven reserves. Taxing foreigners is popular both economically and politically—they do not vote. Of course, domestic oil producers not only vote, they contribute to campaigns, and a tax on gasoline would be unpopular with them. But deals can be made—taxes can be traded for depletion allowances and other accounting goodies to make such a plan politically viable.

A gasoline tax in a small country falls mostly on the residents of that country. The world price of oil is essentially independent of the taxing policies of most countries, since most countries consume only a small fraction of the amount of oil sold. But the United States consumes a lot of oil—almost a quarter of the world's production. That means it has considerable market power: its tax policies have a major impact on the world price of oil, and economic analysis suggests that in the long run, a significant part of a gasoline tax increase would end up being paid by the producers of oil, not the consumers.

Table 9.1.   Paying at the Gas Pump. Source: Energy Information Administration

The price of premium unleaded gasoline may vary around the world, but it is taxes that take the biggest bite in Europe. Average prices shown are for the week ended Oct. 16, 2000.	Cost for a gallon of gas		**Percentage to taxes**	Amount (per gallon) to taxes
	Britain	$4.35	**76.3%**	$3.32
	France	3.50	**68.3**	2.39
	Germany	3.37	**67.5**	2.27
	The Netherlands	3.82	**65.1**	2.49
	Belgium	3.43	**65.0**	2.23
	Italy	3.58	**63.4**	2.27
	United States	1.71	**22.4**	.38

Nearly 20 years ago, Theodore Bergstrom, an economist who is now at the University of California at Santa Barbara, compared the actual petroleum tax policies of various countries with policies those countries would adopt if they wanted to transfer more OPEC profits to themselves. He found that if each major oil-consuming country pursued an independent tax policy, the tax rates in European countries should be somewhat lower than they are now, while the tax rate in the United States should be much higher. If the United States, Europe and Japan all coordinated their oil-tax policies, they would collectively want to impose net tax rates of roughly 100 to 200 percent. This is not as scary as it sounds since such a coordinated tax increase would mostly affect oil producers; the price at the pump would increase much less.

Mr. Bergstrom's analysis was focused entirely on transferring profits from oil-producing to oil-consuming nations. If we factor in the pollution and congestion effects mentioned earlier, the optimal petroleum taxes would be even higher. In the past, Al Gore has advocated increasing gasoline taxes for environmental reasons, though he has been pretty quiet about this proposal lately. George W. Bush does not think much of oil taxes, but he likes the idea of a tax cut.

Let me propose a bipartisan plan: raise the tax on gasoline, but give the revenue back to taxpayers in the form of an income tax credit. Average consumers would be about as well off as they are now, but the higher price of gasoline would tend to discourage consumption—giving us environmental, congestion, and tax-the-foreigner benefits. It would make sense to phase the tax in over several years, so that the next time drivers trade in their sport utility vehicles, they would have an incentive to buy those fuel-efficient cars that Detroit has promised to produce.

Increasing the net tax on gasoline by, say, 2 percent a year for the next 10 years would be pretty painless for most people. Oil prices would almost certainly drop back down in the next few years, tending to reduce the price of gasoline back toward historical levels. A higher gasoline tax would just mean prices would not drop quite as far as they would otherwise.

If something must be taxed, it makes a lot of sense to tax something that is costly to the environment, costly to the users and mostly controlled by foreigners. The United States is passing up a big opportunity by not taxing gasoline at a higher rate. (Varian 2000, C2)

Wow! That is quite a compelling case that Professor Varian makes. Of course, there are many more effects that dramatically raising the price of gasoline will produce—rigid space restrictions prevented Professor Varian from analyzing them, so I'll mention a few.

— All of us will have less money to spend because we pay substantially more for each gallon of gasoline—right? Wrong! Every additional dollar raised in green taxes will be returned to us as income tax reductions. We will have the exact same amount of disposable income after a gas tax increase as before. But how shall we distribute those income tax windfalls? We can do so progressively (e.g., poorer people get more money returned in income tax reductions than they paid in green taxes) or regressively (e.g., all get their taxes reduced by the same percentage) as the body politic determines. However, determining who receives how much in income tax reductions should not keep us from implementing this green tax.

— Will more than doubling the price of gasoline substantially reduce gas consumption and the output of carbon dioxide, nitrogen oxide, sulfur dioxide, and other problem emissions? Absolutely!

— Would profits of the auto companies decline if the price of gasoline were to double? No one can tell for certain. All major automobile makers have high-efficiency models in (or near) production. Some of these models employ internal combustion engines powered by hydrogen, some have all-electric autos, some hybrid electric (e.g., gasoline plus electric battery powered), and all have fuel cell autos on the horizon. The auto companies who get to the market first with the most efficient, reasonably priced models will actually take market share (and likely also increase their profits) at the expense of the laggards. At this time, Honda and Toyota appear to be leading the race, with Daimler-Chrysler closing the gap. However, this is partly due to the fact that the Japanese and European alternative energy autos have competed against high-priced gasoline (due to green taxes) for years. This advantage is largely responsible for their current lead over companies like Ford and General Motors. Implementing a gas tax will at least remove the competitive disadvantage under which American auto companies now labor.

— Surely the oil companies will be against a gas tax! Even this is not completely clear. Some oil companies (such as Exxon-Mobil) are not now aggressively pursuing alternative energy technologies. These companies would probably actively oppose a gasoline tax. However, some oil companies are aggressively investing in alternative energy programs. In several cases (e.g., Chevron-Texaco, Shell-BP) anything (like a gas tax) that moves the world quickly toward the clean and efficient hydrogen economy of the future will give them a competitive advantage over other oil companies, and thus they could actually find a gas tax rather appealing.

— Aren't Europeans and Japanese better able to pay more for gasoline because they have better public transportation systems than does the United States? This brings up an important direction-of-causality problem. Other countries have better public transportation systems *because* they pay more for gasoline. American public transport has become deficient because it could not compete with cheap, subsidized gasoline prices over the last several decades. Raising gasoline prices will be an immediate, significant boon to public transportation—which will then be improved and expanded almost immediately.

— Finally, will green taxes on gasoline reduce traffic jams and make driving fun again? Quite possibly. It depends upon the size of the green tax, how quickly we upgrade public transportation, and that most important other factor—the rate of growth in our population. However, a green tax will surely start us in the direction of decongesting our roads.

— Is there anything better than a green tax on gasoline? Sure is—a carbon tax would be even better! With a carbon tax, all carbon-based energy sources are taxed—not just gasoline. A carbon tax would give American businesses a boost toward leading the world into the (inevitable) solar, wind, and hydrogen technologies of the future. Talk about profoundly changing our futures for the better, a carbon tax might be the death blow to the IRS! Readers now have the intellectual resources to foresee the additional benefits that a carbon tax (on all uses of coal, oil, natural gas, etc.) would have on the world of the future—powered by the clean, renewable, and efficient technologies that American companies (e.g., General Electric, United Technologies, Plug Power, Astro Power, Fuel Cell Inc., Energy Conversion Devices, Chevron-Texaco, Satcon Technologies, Beacon Power, UQM Industries, etc., etc., etc.) might well dominate. I'll leave it to the motivated reader to trace (1) the social outcomes a carbon tax would produce, (2) how it will affect American businesses over the next twenty years, and (3) a wise investment strategy for you to adopt—one that will make you wealthy while facilitating our inevitable transition to the solar/hydrogen economy.

B: Why Are Environmental Decisions So Obvious and Simple in This Book, But So Complex in Political Contexts?

In politics, George, it all comes down to whose ox is being gored.

—My dad

Over time, people have institutionalized wasteful and destructive lifestyles by creating systems (e.g., business, political, educational, legal) that virtually demand that individuals stress their ecosystems. It may be difficult for many readers to appreciate arguments against such basic beliefs as the value of the current so-called "free market" capitalism (Howard 1997). To change human attitudes and behaviors in radical ways, the systems that serve to train and to maintain daily behaviors need to be reengineered. Furthermore, misleading information may move people in the wrong direction.

An Example of Misleading Information

Consider the following startling claim made by Passell (1996):

> Substitute 500,000 electric cars for the same number of new gasoline-powered ones in Los Angeles—a plausible number for the year 2010—and what happens? Not much. Peek levels of ozone are reduced, but only from 200 parts per billion to 199. The current safe level is estimated to be 120 parts per billion, and new research suggests that the target should be lowered to around 70 parts per billion to meet the law's requirement to eliminate all health risk. . . . The fact is, we'd not get any benefit from electric cars. (D2)

This remarkable conclusion is based on research by Lave, Russell, Hendrickson, and McMichael (1996). The claim that ozone levels would be reduced from 200 to 199 parts per billion is true *only* if one assumes that all of Los Angeles's additional electricity will be produced by dirty sources (from natural gas and coal), which was the procedure used to calculate the projected ozone figure of 199. Thus, the source of pollution would simply be moved from tailpipes to electricity-generating plants. However, Los Angeles does not produce electricity solely from polluting sources: Wind, photovoltaic, geothermal, and hydroelectric sources are already being used. With every passing year, more and more of Los Angeles's electricity will be produced by nonpolluting methods (Henderson 1981). In fact, over time the estimate of 199 parts of ozone per billion made by Lave et al. will be more misleading than it already is.

Lave et al.'s (1996) scientific thought experiment represented a fundamentally disingenuous argument from the start. However, it is an exercise that sheds light on the problems of making changes within wasteful systems. In addition to using some highly suspect assumptions and facts (as noted above), Lave et al. asked what would happen if one put a superefficient component (electric cars) into a ghastly, inefficient energy-production system (the current hydrocarbon-based electricity production methods) and then concluded that the immediate results would be disappointing. That is like asking what efficiencies would be obtained if one put a modern, high-performance carburetor into a Model T Ford? If the car would run at all, it surely would not show great efficiencies. Rather than recognizing that society cannot totally redesign an inefficient, polluting energy system overnight and replace it with an efficient, nonpolluting system, Lave et al. incorrectly concluded that society should not change to using electric cars. Massive changes may need to be undertaken piecemeal over long periods of time. The efficiencies of any one component may only be fully realized after other parts of the system also have been improved. However, it is important to adopt long-range time frames (i.e., not to discount the future) when considering such crucial issues. For example, if Los Angeles obtained all of its electricity from less polluting renewable sources (e.g., sunlight, wind, tides, geothermal energy), then the contribution to ozone by 500,000 electric automobiles in Lave et al.'s example would have been roughly zero!

A first step toward reengineering the wasteful power generation system, which is currently incapable of adequately taking advantage of electric cars, would be (as you now know) to initiate a green tax (Hawkin 1993). A green tax would give nonpolluting sources of electricity a chance to gain a greater percentage of the electricity generation market. Green taxes are very versatile tools and represent one of many ways that changes in the U.S. tax system could facilitate environmental reforms.

An Example of Misleading Conclusions

When exposed to global population trends (see Oskamp 2000), many people express surprise that the world population is growing so rapidly. There are several reasons why many people lack a basic awareness of disturbing population trends. The distribution of palliative information by some in U.S. society is one reason. The following example illustrates how technically correct information can be used to promote incorrect conclusions, thus confusing (rather than clarifying) people's understanding of environmental issues.

Students in an environmental psychology course helped write an editorial on the connection between global overpopulation and dwindling grain stocks that was published in the *Chicago Tribune* (Howard 1996). A week after the editorial appeared, an anonymous letter arrived. Inside were four professionally produced pamphlets entitled *World Population Facts*, *Total Fertility Rates Are Plunging Worldwide*, *The World Can Feed Its People*, and *More Grain on Less Land*. These pamphlets were accompanied by a scribbled note that simply said, "Chicken Little—the sky is *not* falling." Messages contained in the four pamphlets were quite consistent with one another. They claimed that, if anything, society ought to worry about there being too few rather than too many people on Earth, and that gains by modern agriculture would be more than able to meet global food demand. Of course, the students were quite disturbed by the disparity between the "facts" offered in these pamphlets and their understanding of trends in population and in food production and consumption.

A senior took it upon himself to find out how the pamphlets' authors could interpret the world population situation so differently than did Ehrlich and Ehrlich (1990), Gore (1992), Howard (1997), Oskamp (2000), and figure 1.1 of this book. The first few lines of the *Total Fertility Rates Are Plunging Worldwide* (no date) pamphlet give the flavor of its message:

> Throughout the world birth rates and total fertility rates are plunging faster and further than ever recorded in human history. Despite all the apocalyptic doomsday predictions of certain overpopulation propagandists, the fact is that population growth in many countries are [sic] already below replacement levels and the world's growth rate is rapidly approaching that figure. (1)

By the end of the pamphlet, a naive reader might be convinced that the species' real threat is this plunging fertility problem rather than overpopulation.

To analyze these claims, the student obtained data from the World Population Profile (U.S. Department of Commerce 1996) revealing that the world population growth rate has declined from 2.0 percent per year during the period of 1960–1970, to 1.8 percent for 1970–1980, to 1.7 percent for 1980–1990. However, the annual increments in global population actually increased during that period from 67 million per year (for the 1960–1970 period) to 75 million per year (for the 1970–1980 period) to 82 million per year (for the 1980–1990 period).

These data show that the pamphlet was technically correct, in that the annual growth rate has been declining since about 1965. However, this fact should not allay fears of overpopulation. Records for increases in the world's total human population continue to be broken year after year, with little prospect for this trend reversing in the foreseeable future. The mathematics of these apparently incompatible truths is really quite simple. Compare the year 1965 with 1997 to see how compatible declining annual growth rates can be with a rapidly increasing human population:

— In 1965: 3.3 billion (population) x 0.021 (growth rate) = 70 million people annual increase (births – deaths).
— In 1997: 5.9 billion (population) x 0.0165 (growth rate) = 92 million people annual increase (births – deaths).

An Example of Misleading Mathematics

Shifting gears a bit, have you been surprised by the amount of mathematics that I've employed in a book that deals with psychology, the environment, and religion? Well, in many ways this book is really about critical thinking—where you believe our world is heading, what's true and false in our lives, what we should believe and why, and so forth. When others try to influence our beliefs (through education, advertisement, propaganda, etc.), they often bolster their arguments with statistics of various sorts. As you've already seen, we need to be extremely cautious in believing what others claim to be true. Oftentimes the most simple mathematical claims are misleading.

Can you be misled with mathematics? We've all heard stories about how acquaintances obtained 25 percent, 50 percent, 100 percent, or even 200 percent gains on their investments. If people are making so much money, why are so many of us strapped financially? Excessive consumption (i.e., spending) undoubtedly is the main problem. No matter how much one earns, if one's expenses increase by the same amount as one's income, that person is going broke. [Because earnings are *decreased* by income (or by capital gains) taxes, while the cost of purchases are *increased* by sales taxes.] However, people are also *systematically misled* by mathematical sleights of hand that lead them to believe that they are doing better financially than they actually are.

Consider this example. The stock market indexes went on a roller-coaster ride recently. A *USA Today* article the next day entitled "Many investors keep their cool" observed, " . . . still [Bridgit] Flavin's tech-heavy stock portfolio . . . is down 30% this year. Isn't she worried? 'Come on. I was up 65% last year,' she says." (April 5, 2000, 5B). The obvious implication being that Bridgit's portfolio is still way up over these rising (65 percent) and declining (30 percent) periods. Let's see if that implication is correct.

Imagine that your $10,000 investment decreased by 50 percent one year and then increased by 50 percent, the next year. Are you back to your initial $10,000 investment? Sorry, you've actually booked a 25 percent loss.

When I show this conundrum to mathematicians or statisticians, many immediately suggest that it might be an artifact of having booked the 50 percent loss first and then taken the 50 percent gain. Would one obtain a different result if the 50 percent gain had been followed by the 50 percent loss? Nope! Your investment declines by 25 percent over the two-year period either way.

Now you tell me—what's the rate of return on Bridgit's investment after a 65 percent gain is followed by a 30 percent loss?

Just to be sure your calculations are correct, imagine that your broker calls and says, "Congratulations! You just made a 90 percent gain on that stock

Table 9.2.

	GAIN FIRST	LOSS FIRST
INITIAL INVESTMENT	$10,000	$10,000
END OF FIRST YEAR	$15,000	$5,000
END OF SECOND YEAR	$7,500	$7,500
RATE OF RETURN OVER 2 YEARS	-25 %	-25 %

that took a 50 percent loss last year." Your reply should be, "Are you in the habit of congratulating people who've lost 5 percent of their money?" Did your calculations yield that counterintuitive truth?

Jane Bryant Quinn makes a similar point in noting, "Here's a lesson in lower math. When a stock drops from $250 to $40, you lose 88 percent of your money. To get back to $250, your stock now has to *gain* 733 percent (*Newsweek*, December 25, 2000, 69).

Perhaps we've allowed ourselves to be misled as to how well we've done financially by similar mathematical sleights of hand. As a psychologist, I know that one's willingness to be misled by overly optimistic statistics is related to the more general human tendency to think that our futures will be rosy. Perhaps we would all do well to be more realistic about our future prospects—financial and otherwise.

What does this little exercise say about our view of the environmental crises that now confront us? Much of what I read in the press about environmental problems sounds a lot like "We gained 20 percent of X last year, and lost 15 percent of X this year—we're making progress!" Unfortunately, virtually all of the experts who bother to dig beneath the surface statistics come away deeply troubled by present environmental trends. Now you tell me, who captures this reality better—the simple statistics or the professionals who dig beneath the surface? For those who vote for the simple statistics, I've got some shares of a bridge in Brooklyn that you might like to purchase. Because you're my friend, I'm willing to sell them to you at the ridiculously low price of ———.

C: The Science of Ovonics: Is It Really an Environmentalist's Dream-Come-True?

Why did the American Chemical Society designate Stan and Iris Ovshinsky as "Heroes of Chemistry?" They were honored for their contributions to the science of ovonics. But what has ovonics to do with the environment—and what do the Ovshinskys teach us about the role that dreams play in creating a better future?

The Oxford English Dictionary (1989) defines *Ovonic* as

(in the name of Stanford R. Ovshinsky [(b. 1922)], the U.S. physicist and industrialist who discovered the property). Pertaining to, involving, or utilizing the property of certain amorphous semi-conductors of making a rapid, reversible transition from a non-conducting to a conducting state on the application of an electric field stronger than some minimum value. Hence ovonics (*pl.*), the study and application of ovonic effects and devices.

The Ovshinskys are to ovonics what Mendel was to genetics and what Darwin was to evolution. Environmentalists hope that a decade from now ovonics will be producing the practical achievements that genetics, for example, is now beginning to deliver. In 1955, Stan Ovshinsky discovered the fundamental principles of disordered and amorphous materials (known as the "Ovshinsky effect") that served as the basis for the science of ovonics—which specializes in the creation and development of new materials that possess characteristics capable of handling important practical problems.

Consider the Ovshinskys' vision of a hydrogen-powered future for automobiles. Enormous amounts of energy reach the earth each day as sunlight. Photovoltaic collectors (in the form of shingles and standing roofs on homes, commercial buildings, parking garages, etc.) convert the sun's light into electricity. This electricity can then be employed to produce hydrogen and oxygen gases (via the hydrolysis of water). Hydrogen is rocket fuel—which is dangerous in both its gaseous and liquid states. Fortunately, Texaco Ovonics safely stores 7 percent (by weight) hydrogen in a solid alloy (a metal hydride). A hydrogen tank of such metal hydrides (in an automobile) stores enough hydrogen to cover about 300 miles, when the hydrogen is used as the fuel to be burned in a standard internal combustion engine. When employed with an Ovonic Regenerative Fuel Cell and an Ovonic Nickel Metal Hydride Battery, the range of the car is extended well beyond 300 miles on a single tank of hydrogen. Why does this hydrogen-based energy system represent a singular environmental achievement?

Even when burned in an internal combustion engine, hydrogen produces *no pollutants* and none of the climate change effects of carbon-based fuels. Thus, it is an environmentalist's dream fuel! This characteristic would be impressive enough in itself, but think of how hydrogen will be *produced* in the Ovshinskys' total vision of a hydrogen-powered economy. Rather than drilling for oil in Alaska's Arctic National Wildlife Refuge (ANWR), transporting oil to refineries via *Exxon Valdez*–type supertankers, and blanketing communities with refineries' toxic pollutants (like Bayway, N.J., Gary, Ind., and Baytown, Tex.—to name just three communities that I've lived near), one merely collects energy anywhere the sun shines in a totally nonpolluting, completely renewable fashion. This energy is then transformed into hydrogen on site and used to perform work—all of which occurs without any pollution. Of course, the OPEC nations will not be pleased with the thought of every American family and business collecting most of their energy needs each day (free of charge) from our bountiful sun.

Consider the economics of the Ovshinskys' dream for an individual family. The sun shines upon your roof made up of Ovonic Photovoltaic Shingles each morning and immediately begins recharging your home's Ovonic Nickel Metal Hydride Batteries, which are a bit low because of your use of lights, electric appliances, heat (or air conditioning), and the regeneration overnight of your car's Ovonic batteries and/or fuel cells. All day, as you work or play, your roof is producing the fuel you'll need later that day. However, on sunny days you generate no electricity bill, no natural gas bill, and no gasoline charges! This modern-day miracle (which was only a futurist's dream a few years ago) has now been demonstrated via commercial-scale production products.

Initially, ovonics looked to hold more promise for developing new forms of computer memory and optical storage devices than it appeared to hold for a hydrogen future. [ECD now has joint ventures with Intel on computer memory (Ovonyx, Inc.) and with General Electric on optical storage devices (Ovonic Media, LLC) to pursue these information-based applications of ovonic science.] However, in 1960, when the Ovshinskys founded Energy Conversion Devices (ECD), their vision of the hydrogen economy dominated the company's development from the beginning. As Robert Stempel (the former chairman of General Motors and now ECD's CEO) puts it, "Stan actually built the company based on hydrogen. From the very first days in 1960, he knew that hydrogen would be an important part of the future of the world."

Stempel continues, "ECD is a materials company. We're changing the crystalline structure of matter to perform important tasks. That's key—and that's what ECD does very well. We follow Stan Ovshinsky's atomic engineering principle. The secret is to tailor elements from the periodic table to achieve a variety of different properties in these alloys. For example, in our battery materials, we had three properties in mind: (1) 7% (by weight) storage, (2) high charging kinetics, and (3) very long cycle life."

In order to tell a simple story of the Ovshinskys' dream of the coming hydrogen economy, I was forced to gloss over several very thorny engineering problems. For example, the hydrolysis of water into hydrogen and oxygen gases required too much electricity to be a commercially feasible process—

until ECD developed proprietary catalytic materials that together with its amorphous thin-film photovoltaics could increase the efficiency and decrease the cost of electrolytically generating hydrogen from water and storing it as needed in its proprietary magnesium-based alloys.

Similarly, the Proton Exchange Membrane (PEM) fuel cell was the leading candidate to drive hydrogen-powered automobiles. Internal combustion engines are about 25 percent efficient, whereas PEMs are about 40 percent efficient. ECD's Ovonic Regenerative fuel cell is about 60 percent efficient. Further, PEMs require expensive noble metals whereas ECD developed much less expensive, non-noble metals as substitutes for their fuel cell. Over the course of more than forty years, the Ovshinskys have solved the scientific, technological, and engineering hurdles that stood in the way of their dream of a seamless, hydrogen system (from sunlight to a Sunday drive). ECD believes that they are building the energy system of the future.

Unfortunately, the world was not ready for the hydrogen economy in the 1960s, or in the 1970s, or 1980s, or 1990s. Thus, ECD has run up an astounding forty years of almost uninterrupted business losses. Nevertheless, the ECD team pressed on toward their hydrogen vision undeterred. For good historical reason, Wall Street now gives the company little respect (i.e., its stock is currently in the mid-teens, which is a level the stock first reached almost thirty years ago). Still, a loyal band of investors (and an even more loyal band of talented ECD employees) have until now been denied the success of profitability in their pursuit of the dream of a clean, renewable hydrogen future. As part of its long-standing strategy, ECD has made investments in its technologies that have resulted in enabling intellectual property and products which, under Generally Accepted Accounting Principles (GAAP), have to be reported as losses. ECD has recently entered into strategic alliances and joint ventures with some of the world's leading corporations, thus forming the basis to commercialize its products. The bulk of its assets consist of intellectual property and patents. Under GAAP, these types of assets are not recognizable on its balance sheet.

Shifting gears, did you know that $1.6 million of Notre Dame's endowment is invested by business majors in a course, entitled "Applied Investment Management?" Each year fifty to sixty companies are thoroughly researched, and the class votes on a few new companies to be added to the university's portfolio. In the fall of 2000, eight companies were added. ECD received the second most positive class vote of the fifty-six companies reviewed, and ECD is now a holding in Notre Dame's endowment. Were our students voting with their hearts or their heads in selecting ECD?

Rick Buhrman, then the captain of Notre Dame's tennis team, argued ECD's case before the court of his classmates. Rick maintained that ECD made perfect sense to both the heart and the head. "Will forty years of losses matter if ECD becomes the General Electric or the Microsoft of the twenty-first century?" he asks. "The company—and its forty years of losses—actually wasn't a very hard sell. After all, this jury's members had all chosen to attend a school that sees a crucifixion as a necessary step to a resurrection. We're willing to risk financial death—if the cause is right. And frankly, buying forty years of valuable intellectual property (over 350 U.S. patents, and over 800 corresponding foreign patents) for pennies on the dollar minimizes our risk rather dramatically." Apparently, his classmates found Rick's arguments compelling.

The Ovshinskys and ECD have held fast to their dream of a hydrogen-powered future. They will be the heroes of this contemporary morality play—should the outcome go well. While they certainly don't need Notre Dame's help, they are always happy to see their stock in the hands of fellow dreamers. Frankly, I doubt that any in the ECD family would complain if their stock were now to become the recipient of some of our famous "luck of the Irish." All investors and ECD employees who lend their support in this noble effort will be entitled to take a bow—and a handsome profit also—for their part in giving birth to a dream of a better future for our planet and its ecosystems.

Waking dreams are important phenomena that psychology has largely ignored for too long. Environmentally concerned citizens everywhere will be delighted when the Ovshinskys' long-deferred dream explodes into reality. However, deferred dreams can sometimes have a dark side. Thinking of race relations, Langston Hughes observed, "What happens to a dream deferred? Does it dry up, like a raisin in the sun—or does it explode?" The ending of ECD's dream will soon become known—here's hoping it's an explosion of celebration and vindication for the Ovshinskys' Herculean efforts.

~

PART THREE

Against the Idols of Our Day

Since my father's death, I've been thinking a lot about spirit. While no one would describe my dad as a religious person, he was often characterized as a spiritual man. He never thought himself superior to others, as he possessed a genuine liking and caring for people. Don't get me wrong, there were definitely ways that one could "get on his bad side." However, in the course of his life, few ever suffered that fate. I think this is because my father genuinely enjoyed both his life and the people in it. My dad also had a basic love of nature and the outdoor life that I could only vaguely understand. He caught more fish and just missed shooting more birds and mammals (deer, turkey, pheasant, rabbit, squirrel, raccoon, opossum, etc.) than any human I'll ever know. His love of fishing and hunting was not at all surprising, since he steadfastly maintained that his earliest memory of his mother was watching her crawl over a hill on her belly to get a better shot at a woodchuck. [They just don't make mothers like that anymore!]

Readers who have strong emotional and/or philosophical objections to killing animals will always have insuperable difficulties in appreciating how my father understood the natural world and the place of humans as just another species among many in the animal kingdom. He was as comfortable killing and eating other species as he would have been being killed and eaten by a bear or a shark. Think about that statement! For my dad, it was an honor to be able to play one's role in the natural order—whatever that role might be. Despite my father's unending efforts to educate me in his vision of the place of humans in nature, it remains for me a foreign vision of the web of life—as incomprehensible as most foreign languages.

My father was "connected" to nature in ways that I will never be. At one level I understood his worldview, but it always remained somebody else's belief system—not reality as I knew it. Happily, my cousin Rich Jones was my father's spiritual son. Over time, they grew to become like two peas in a pod. I never resented Rich's special relationship with my dad, because I always got whatever I needed from my parents. Rich and my father saw the world "through the same eyes." It's always nice to find someone who loves what you love, someone who values what you value.

Noethe (2000) conducted extensive interviews with twenty-one of the leading environmentalists and conservationists in the country. He found that the majority of people, who work heroically toward blunting the impact of emerging environmental threats, have a profound connection to nature. In that respect, they are more like my father than they are like me. Further, environmental activists typically volunteer a particular early-life experience (or a particular place) where they formed this emotional bond to the natural world. Almost as often, they can cite a specific experience that dramatized for them the perils that our planet's ecosystems now face. For such people, their love of nature becomes an important part of the spiritual backdrop upon which their environmental activism is built. I discussed my father because his form of spirituality owed almost nothing to religious traditions. The book of "nature's ways" was his only sacred text. My father knew the book of nature as well as any person I'll ever know. This familiarity enabled him to walk as gently upon the earth as any member of our overly materialistic, consumption-fixated society is able. But I worry about our society's future, in part because all of my father's children and grandchildren were raised in artificial environments—cities. People like my father grow scarcer with each passing day.

On the other hand, many environmentally concerned people find their way to environmentally appropriate beliefs and lifestyles through the tenets of organized religions. The final section of this book seeks to articulate the ways that a few religious traditions have fostered beliefs and lifestyles that will make our species less of a burden on the earth and its ecosystems in the twenty-first century.

The first chapter of part III deals with "The Common Good," which is an important element of most religious traditions. Solving the environmental challenges before us demands that we give greater weight to the good of the group—rather than what is in our own self-interest—if we are to reverse present disturbing trends. The Christian tradition is probed in chapter 11 entitled "It Is Easier for a Camel. . . ." Christianity's traditional distrust of extreme wealth and its preference for ascetic, communal lifestyles offer powerful resources as we move away from materialist values toward lives focused upon spiritual values. Sadly, the Catholic Church's current opposition to all artificial methods of birth control makes the church less than helpful in the struggle against global overpopulation and the misery it creates. Eastern spiritual traditions are searched for nuggets of environmental wisdom in chapters 12 and 13, entitled "Buddhist Economics" and "Gandhi's Seven Sins" respectively. Finally, the religiously inspired keys for the earth-friendly beliefs and lifestyles of the twenty-first century are summarized in the final chapter entitled "Changing Human Societies."

~

CHAPTER TEN

In Praise of the Common Good

For whatever reasons, religious traditions tend to focus attention upon the group rather than on individuals. Jews are "the chosen people." Christians are the "people of god," and thus among the saved. In Buddhist thought, "all is the Tao, and the Tao is all." One's spiritual challenge, then, is "to become one with the Tao." Over and over, we find evidence that God's pact is with a group—not with individuals.

Similarly, with rare exceptions such as Calvinism, religious traditions tend to be suspicious of too much wealth and try to promote various forms of asceticism—voluntary simplicity, self-denial, etc. For this reason, religious traditions often find themselves in conflict with the materialism, consumerism, and individualism that now permeates contemporary First World societies. Thus, if one fears the environmental problems that now seem to be upon us, various religious traditions can be seen as valuable resources in constructing solutions to our pressing environmental dilemmas.

Ecological Sanity

Imagine there is a beautiful water lily that doubles in number each day. You live on a lake, but you don't notice when the first water lily establishes itself in a remote inlet of the lake (Day 1 = 1 lily). You first notice this gorgeous flower when it still covers less than one percent of your lake's surface. Assume that if left unchecked, the plant will eventually cover the entire lake in one month (31 days)—thereby killing all other life forms. At that point in time there will be 1.073 billion lilies, which will surely overwhelm the lake's ecosystems. When would be the latest day of the month that you might take action against this biological menace, and still allow your lake a fighting chance to repel the intruder? Would you act when the plant covers 25 percent of the lake? Fifty percent of the lake? Eighty percent? Ninety-five percent? Exactly how long could you wait to act?

If you chose to act when the lake was half covered with lilies, you left only one day—and thus no margin for error—to act. This is because the lake is half full with lilies at the end of the thirtieth day of the month—and completely dead 24 hours later!

The point of this exercise is to dramatize the fact, first discussed in chapter 1, that when projecting trends into the future, humans tend to think in terms of constant increases (i.e., arithmetic progressions). This assumption about the nature of growth serves us well in some instances. For example, if I put $10 under my pillow each day for a month (31 days) I'll have $310 at the end of the month. When will I have half that amount—on day 15 or day 30?

One can see from these two examples that if one simply did not notice that the water lily example represented a case of geometric growth, then waiting until the lake was half full before acting might suggest (incorrectly) that one still had about half a month to defeat the biotic intruder. While this assumption would have been correct if the lily grew arithmetically, it can lead to disastrous consequences when growth is geometric. Geometric growth rates start slowly (e.g., after the first ten days there would still only be 512 lilies). However, once geometric growth processes begin to gain momentum the time left to react can be extremely short (e.g., 536,870,880 new lilies were added to the lake on the last day of the month). Are there any examples of geometric growth rates in nature?

Presumably, all species of biological organisms grow geometrically until constraints (i.e., food supply, waste products, lack of territory, increases in predators) end their geometric growth. Figure 1.1 in chapter 1 presents the geometric growth in society's favorite biological organism (*homo sapiens*) over the past 1,000 years. One can easily see that we are well into the accelerated growth phase of geometric increase in the human population. While it took roughly one million years for humans to reach the first billion in population, and another 117 years (1810–1927) to add the second billion, adding the most recent billion required only 12 years (1987–1999). Because we are dealing with geometric growth, the time left to deal with the explosive increases in the human population is short indeed. Other examples of "natural" phenomena that grow geometrically are debt (e.g., unpaid balances on charge cards, the national debt) and untaxed compounded savings (e.g., IRAs, SEPs, Keoghs) as you saw in chapter 6. So great was Albert Einstein's respect for geometric growth that he once claimed, "The most powerful thing man ever invented is compounded interest" (Merrill Lynch 1997, 9).

My choice to transform a "beautiful water lily" into an omniverous aquatic plague was intentional. For millennia we have been taught that humans represent both the apex of evolution and the creation that reflects God's own image and likeness. In a relatively short period of time (a century), humans have gone from being creation's crowning glory to being a blight upon the earth. How could we have fallen so far so fast?

The speed of our fall from grace does *not* speak to any rapid changes in humans themselves. Rather, it reflects the impact that geometric increases in the human population has had on a planet that has not grown in millennia. We are now thrown up against important *limits* in life. Because our thinking developed in an underpopulated world of abundant natural resources and underused waste sinks, many human beliefs are simply unfit for our world of six billion people.

For example, people have long believed that if something is good, then more of that thing is an even better situation. We rather uncritically accept that growth (or progress, or development) represents a desirable circumstance. Thus, an economy must be growing in order to be considered healthy. Stable economies are labeled as "stagnant" and even some growing economies (e.g., 1 to 3 percent growth per year) are considered to be underperforming. Not long ago, in the year 2000, one routinely heard investors derided because their safe investments were yielding "only" about 7 percent returns.

Humans must now learn to desire stasis and to distrust growth in many areas of their lives. Unfortunately, virtually all Western belief systems are based upon notions of progress, growth, and development. Contemporary economics is so indoctrinated in the growth-is-good belief that the economist E. F. Schumacher recommended "Buddhist economics" as an antidote for our dominant modes of economic thought (Schumacher 1973). However, Schumacher's ideas are still so foreign to the idols of Western economic systems that they appear to have had no impact upon mainstream practitioners of "the dismal science." Thus, chapter 12 will address Buddhist thought as it applies to the domains of economics and psychology.

An Allegory of Two Teams

Once upon a time [actually, one occurred just before the close of the last millennium, the other at the dawn of the new millennium] there were two teams [actually, one was a high school Lacrosse team, the other was a grammar school basketball team] whose "star player," during the heat of battle, lashed out at his younger, less-skilled teammates, as he was replaced midway through a game where our team was falling farther and farther behind our more talented opponents. The coach [actually, me in both cases] had two goals in mind in making the substitution. First, I believe that "If something isn't working, try something else." [Actually, I learned this maxim twenty-five years ago in my training as a psychotherapist. Later, Phil Jackson (1995) confirmed my belief, that opponents can't help but drop their guard when they see "the subs" enter the game. This loss of intensity often allows our second-teamers to shock the opponent (by scoring some points and reducing their lead). If our team then substitutes in our rested and revivified (because of the energy generated by seeing our second-teamers outscore their starters) starters, our opponents are faced with a terrible decision. Do they hope their tired (and now perhaps shaken) first string can stave off our rested and revivified first string? Or do they trust their second string to stem the tide against our starters? Jackson never sees replacing his starters as "giving up." Rather, substitutions always represent strategic coaching moves. Does this strategy always work? Hardly! But in both stories, our starters were already falling farther behind—and, as you know, when things aren't working. . . .] My second goal in substituting was plain, good old-fashioned fairness to the second-stringers—to kids who'd worked hard in practice but not yet been rewarded by playing in this game. As you'll see in chapter 12, some form of fairness to all ought to be a coaching goal—at least it should from a Buddhist perspective.

Unfortunately, in both the basketball and Lacrosse stories, the "stars" loudly claimed that putting in the subs meant that we were "giving up." For second-teamers it's difficult to give their best effort for the team's common good when their own teammates think they can't succeed. If only the starters (in both examples) had instead implored, "Come on, guys. Score some points. Pick us up. Get us back in this game." Would that motivate a second-stringer to his or her best efforts? I think it would.

Unfortunately, in both stories, we lost the game by substantial margins and everyone—starters, substitutes, coach—felt badly for their part in the debacle. In fact, in the basketball example, that loss set the tone for the remainder of the season—more losses, lots more anger, no one feeling supported or appreciated, and so forth. Everyone realized that no one was sacrificing for the common good—so everyone viewed the remainder of the season from their own, self-centered perspective. No one thought first about the good of the team. Finally, we all heaved a sigh of relief as the last loss ended our basketball season. One can only stand so much ego-centeredness.

However, things went differently in the Lacrosse story. The angry star player calmly explained why his frustration led him to lash out at the coach and his teammates. Then we discussed whether it was a wise strategic move to substitute at that point in a game (still a risky, debatable point) and whether the player's reaction was helpful (no matter how understandable it was) to teammates and coaches. This "clearing of the air" helped to improve the atmosphere on the Lacrosse team and they finished as one of the top teams in the state.

My sports allegory is meant to suggest that individualistic thinking— rather than being self-sacrificing for the good of the group—often leads to disastrous outcomes for all members of the group. Sadly, years ago (when I was growing up) youth sports programs were the domains where kids learned to sacrifice for the good of the team. But then Vince Lombardi said that winning was more than everything: it was the only thing. And stupidly, many believed him. What does this lesson have to say about the global ecological problems we now face? First, imagine you are a 21-year-old who grew up in a large, happy family. And now you wish to start a large, happy family of your own. With the image of that young adult in mind, read this chapter's summary. Second, the relationship between what's good for an individual and what's good for the group needs to be rethought.

From Benevolent Invisible Hands to Commons Tragedies

Adam Smith's analogy of markets—that function like benevolent invisible hands—guided the bulk of Western economic thinking for several hundred years. What's good for an individual will also be good for society in the aggregate, Smith's analogy suggested. This invisible hand of the market enabled people to rationalize strategies that other wisdom systems (e.g., most religions) explicitly decried—such as "greed is good."

However, in the closing decades of the twentieth century, we were confronted with more and more cases where unbridled self-interest led to tragedies rather than the betterment of all, as the invisible hand analogy suggested. Garrett Hardin (1968) in "The Tragedy of the Commons" gave the best analogy for the new relationship between individual actions and the common good for the twenty-first century. In a world characterized by severe limits, growth, maximization, development, and greed are often destructive impulses that serve to undermine the common good. More and more, wise individuals are those who recognize when "enough is enough." And such decisions are no longer to be based upon the answer to the question "Would I be better off if I _____ (e.g., had one more child, purchased a gas-guzzling auto)?" Rather, the moral citizen of the twenty-first century is urged to see potential "commons tragedies" everywhere. She or he should frequently asks questions like "How goes it for the world, if every person _____ (e.g., has a large family, drives a gas-guzzling auto)?" This shift in perspective leads to quite a different morality than the *homo economicus* envisioned by Adam Smith. Humans, who are defined primarily as stewards of the commons, exhibit lifestyles that are very similar to the forms of voluntary simplicity and asceticism endorsed by most ancient religions.

Finally, a government that saw its role as aiding citizens in their struggle to protect the commons, would implement green taxes and eschew subsidies that encouraged greater consumption of carbon-based energy sources. You can see we still have a long way to go in the United States—both as individuals and as a political whole.

Can there be a healthy tree in a sick forest? There certainly can be—in the short run. However, in the long run, whatever it is that is killing the rest of the forest's trees will probably overtake the currently healthy individual tree. For a variety of reasons late-twentieth-century humans have turned their attention and concern away from the health of the collectives of which they are members and focused doggedly upon their own health as individuals. Robert Bellah and his co-authors (1985) claim that the first language of American moral life has become *self-reliant individualism*. There are second languages that we also know—the languages of tradition and commitment. However, these second languages are called into use *only* "when the language of the radically separate self does not seem adequate" (20–21). In the first language of self-reliant individualism, one need not even worry about the health of the rest of the forest—it is enough to know that the individual tree is doing fine. However, in the second languages, the health of the community represents a *precondition* for any individual to be healthy. My college class recently held its twenty-fifth anniversary reunion. If I asked every classmate, "how are you doing financially?" they'd all think of their (individual) assets if they chose to reply to my impolite query. Would anyone ever think to reply in the second language and say, "Terrible! We're almost $5 trillion in debt!"? Exactly how valuable will your wealth (e.g., stocks, bonds, insurance policies, homes) be if we (collectively) go bankrupt?

Can a Child Grow Up Healthy in a Toxic Environment?

Too much human activity can pollute (e.g., garbage, liquid wastes, carbon dioxide) a physical environment. But humans live in more environments than just their physical environments. My family, my job, my local community, and my nation also represent social environments in which I live. Can a social environment also be polluted?

James Garbarino (1995) in *Raising Children in a Socially Toxic Environment* wrote, "What I mean by the term *socially toxic environment* is that the social world of children, the social context in which they grow up, has become poisonous to their development" (4). Social toxicity is meant to parallel the physical toxicity that now threatens the survival and well-being of many biological species. Garbarino then identifies

> the social equivalents of lead and smoke in the air, PCBs in the water, and pesticides in the chain. They're easy enough to identify: violence, poverty and other economic pressures on parents and their children, disruptions of relationships, despair, depression paranoia, alienation—all of the things that demoralize families and communities. (4–5)

"Not to worry," I thought, as I read the characteristics of a toxic social environment. "My kids aren't depressed or alienated. Nor are they the victims of violence, or drugs, or a broken home, or bad schools, or. . . ." And then I caught myself. I was thinking individualistically. Sooner or later our toxic social environment will extract a toll on all children—mine included. Can a healthy tree go unscathed in a dying forest?

Garbarino then depicts how much more dangerous it is to grow up in the 1990s than it was for him growing up in the 1960s.

> When I was in high school in the 1960s, I used to write an opinion column for the school newspaper. One month I wrote an article criticizing the fraternities at my school, an act that angered many of my peers. As a result, late one night a car pulled up and dumped garbage on the lawn of our house: I was the victim of a drive-by *littering*.
>
> Today, in many communities, the consequences of making your adolescent peers mad at you might be a drive-by shooting instead of a pile of garbage on your lawn. The same behavior that thirty years ago produced a rather benign form of intimidation might today get you killed. This insight started me thinking about the many ways in which the social environment for kids today is more dangerous than it was when I was growing up. *Drugs:* There was no crack cocaine available to troubled kids then. *Violence:* It was almost unheard of for a teenage bully to have a gun. *AIDS:* We were warned off sex, but no one said

we would die from it. *Television:* The content of television programs was bland and innocuous by today's standards. *Family instability:* Most families had two parents and could afford to live on one income.

These thoughts led me to the concept of the socially toxic environment, the idea that the mere act of living in our society today is dangerous to the health and well-being of children and adolescents. (Garbarino 1995, ix–x, emphasis in original)

Do you know how metaphors work in science? Neils Bohr used our understanding of the sun and the planets in our solar system to help scientists imagine what the relationship of the atom's nucleus and its electrons might be. For over fifty years, Bohr's model of the atom served as a scientifically fruitful metaphor. In a metaphor, a scientist takes a well-accepted or well-understood phenomenon (e.g., the structure of our solar system) and invites other scientists to increase their understanding of a poorly understood phenomenon (e.g., the structure of the atom) by noting similarities between the two. Garbarino feels that the ecological decline and toxicity of our physical environment is so apparent, well understood, and accepted that it can serve as the base metaphor for the emerging toxic social environment with which our children must also deal. Parts of this book deal with concrete ways that we might strive to arrest the decline and increasing toxicity of our physical environment. Such decline must be halted before we can begin to think about paths toward sustainable development. The definition of sustainable development is development that meets the needs of the present without compromising the ability of future generations to meet their needs (Schmidheiny 1992). Thus, halting deterioration in our environment represents the first step (a precondition) before sustainable development can become a possibility.

Garbarino (1995) points out that we are short-changing our children by asking them to grow up in socially toxic environments (e.g., crime, drugs, family instability), just as we are short-changing them by leaving them a degraded, toxic, physical environment. Improving the social and physical environments in which our children will develop will require both more money and greater commitment of our time and energy. Sadly, these demands come at a time when societal pressures and our current lifestyles make money and time extremely scarce commodities for most adults. However, if we do not soon break current trends and invest more time and money in our children, we will have squandered our other (along with our planet) most important natural resource.

The old metaphors—self-contained individuals, invisible hands—created a world that is becoming more physically and socially toxic with each passing day. Those metaphors are incapable of reversing present trends, and returning our physical and social ecosystems to health. We must, instead, entertain more helpful metaphors—some old (like religious notions of the common good) and some new (like Garrett Hardin's commons tragedies) to reverse the terrible problems caused by too many humans living unsustainable lifestyles.

Summary

This chapter depicted how moral and religious belief systems tend to see the common good as an important value. In the nineteenth and twentieth centuries we saw the continual growth in various "goods" (e.g., people, GDP, wealth, consumables) as also serving this common good. And, back then, in an underpopulated world, what was good for an individual was generally good for the group also. But because we now live in a world of strict limits (e.g., nonrenewable natural resources, finite amounts of undeveloped land, overstressed waste sinks), the common good will more often be served by stasis and decline in human numbers and their "wants and needs." The destruction of the earth's ecosystems is caused by the (often geometrically) increasing size of the human footprint on our globe. As a mature species, we must first learn to value stasis, and then to appreciate a decline in our species numbers and also the environmental destructiveness of the consumption patterns that now scar our planet. Why is it important for our common good that humans choose to have a smaller impact on ecosystems, you may ask? Almost forty years ago, Paul Ehrlich gave an answer that is far more true now, then it was when he penned it. You'll recall Ehrlich's answer from chapter 5 on maximization. It bears repeating, as much as does Jeremiah's warnings to the people of Israel.

> In summary, the world's population will continue to grow as long as the birth rate exceeds the death rate; it's as simple as that. When it [the world's population] stops growing or starts to shrink, it will mean that either the birth rate has gone down or the death rate has gone up or a combination of the two. Basically, then, there are only two kinds of solution to the population problem. One is a "birth rate solution," in which we find ways to lower the birth rate. The other is a "death rate solution," in which ways to raise the death rate—war, famine, pestilence—find us. The problem could have been avoided by population control, in which mankind consciously adjusted the birth rate so that the "death rate solution" did not have to occur. (Ehrlich 1968, 34–35)

It is now completely clear that the common good is served by *less*—not more—human beings. Will leveling or reducing the growth rate of the human population by a "birth rate solution" conflict with Western, individualistic ideas about personal freedom? Absolutely! Then have we reached an impasse of conflicting values with no intellectual resources to adjudicate this dispute? To some thinkers—yes; to members of religious traditions—absolutely not!

To Buddhists, for example, extreme positions (such as having no children or having as many children as one wants) are always suspect options, and generally to be avoided. The middle way (e.g., one, two, or three children) is likely the path to Nirvana. Similarly, summarizing a long line of Western (e.g., Aristotle) and Christian (e.g., Thomas Acquinas) thought, Jacques Maritain (1931) draws the following, remarkable "tie-breaker" rule when weighing opposing value choices, "the good of the whole is *more divine* than the good of the parts" (p. 29, emphasis in original). Thus, Christians are urged to prefer the common good to their own self-interest, in moral deliberations where individual and group "goods" are in conflict. Once again, religious perspectives find themselves at war with the idols of our day. Unless we learn to think more for the common good than for our own, individual self-interest, I'm afraid that our fate (both as a species and as individuals) is sealed and ominous.

CHAPTER ELEVEN

∿

It Is Easier for a Camel . . .

"It is easier for a camel to go through the eye of the needle than for someone who is rich to enter the kingdom of God" (Mark 10:25). Wealth is problematic from a Christian perspective.

This chapter will speak to the relationship between the environmental movement and Christian traditions. The modern environmental movement gained great momentum shortly after Rachel Carson's publication of *Silent Spring* in 1962. Soon thereafter (1967), in a very widely discussed article, the cultural historian Lynn White Jr. claimed that the Christian tradition was the world's most anthropocentric religious tradition. White blamed Western technology's exploitative relationship with nature on its (largely) Judeo-Christian heritage. Thus, the early discussion of the role of Christianity in the environmental crisis was adversarial and unproductive. Certainly, if one focused upon a few isolated scriptural quotes (e.g., "let them [humankind] have dominion over the earth" [Genesis 1:26]; "Be fruitful and multiply, and fill the earth and subdue it" [Genesis 1:28]), one might see support for White's thesis. However, I believe that all such attempts to cast blame for current environmental problems on any group or belief system are ultimately counterproductive.

Happily, there is much in the Judeo-Christian tradition that is pro-environment. In fact, rather than quibbling over the meaning of isolated quotes, many now work to develop and refine entire theological systems that see humans' proper relationship to the environment as a basis for a Christian theology. A brief review of four general types of Christian theologies of the environment will give a sense of the great many ways that Christian traditions might buttress proenvironmental attitudes, lifestyles, and spiritualities.

Arguments against White's thesis resulted in the notion of "stewardship" as a viable alternative to White's belief that Christianity advocates "dominion" of humans over nature. Douglas Hall (1986, 1990) then offered stewardship as one of three roles for the Christian: steward, priest, and poet. The steward symbol comes from both biblical texts and long-standing church traditions. Stewardship implies solidarity, accountability, and responsibility— all suggesting a caring leadership by humans. However, even this notion of stewardship seems overly hierarchical to a group of "process theologians" (e.g., John Cobb 1972, 1982; Jay McDaniel 1989, 1990; Catherine Keller 1986, 1996) who want to see humans *only* as an element in the grand scheme of nature, rather than as a "steward over" nature.

A second group of Christian theologians, often called the new cosmologists, offer a second, environmentally sensitive approach to Christians' self-understanding.

[T]he new cosmology is a scientifically informed mythic narrative of the origin and integration of the universe, stars, solar systems, the earth, humans, and life itself. It is an attempt to portray "the big picture" of creation, amalgamating recent scientific data and mythical and religious sensibilities, all with an eye toward discerning the proper place of the human within the cosmos. For the new cosmologists there is no more grand or important story to relate.

New cosmology asserts that popular and religious understandings of the universe have not kept pace with twentieth century scientific discoveries. The universe as cosmos (a given, fully formed, static entity) has been replaced in scientific understanding by the notion of cosmogenesis (the universe as an emerging, dynamic, and integral phenomenon containing a distinctive narrative). New cosmology attempts to help people, including scientists and theologians, relate this emergence to religious and ecological consciousness. (Scharper 1998, 111)

Thomas Berry, a Passionist priest, actually refers to himself as a "Geologian." By that he means that the traditional, Catholic sources of revelation (sacred scripture, the history of the church, personal experience) should be complemented by the story of the cosmos as a fourth source of divine revelation. Thus, the looming environmental catastrophes should be viewed as a contemporary, dire message from God to his people, just as Jeremiah delivered God's rebuke to the chosen people thousands of years ago. The new cosmologists offer a methodological challenge to Christian theologians, in the same way that part I of this book used current environmental problems (overpopulation and overconsumption) to determine a set of important psychological issues (short-term focus, perfectionism, extremism, individualism, etc.) for psychologists to tackle. Similarly, in part II, systemic problems (e.g., "free market" systems that encourage overconsumption, carbon-based energy systems, institutional stimulants to overpopulation) were identified that challenge politicians, businessmen, economists, religious leaders, etc., to rethink the social, economic, and business institutions that impel humans toward environmental destruction. The recent, terrifying round of developments in the evolution of the cosmos signal, for Berry and the other new cosmologists, the nature of our latest spiritual challenge—to create a livable, ecozoic (ecologically appropriate) future for our universe, rather than continuing on our nightmare journey toward a technozoic era.

A third group of Christian theologians, who glean revelatory wisdom from the looming environmental crises, are called ecofeminist theologians. These thinkers (e.g., Rosemary Radford Ruether 1975, 1983; Sallie McFague 1987, 1993; Vandana Shiva 1989, 1991) see environmental problems as one of the many spawn of the sickness of patriarchy, "Racism, sexism, class exploitation, and ecological destruction are four interlocking pillars upon which the structure of patriarchy rests" (Collins, 1974).

The fourth group, liberation theologians (e.g., Leonardo Boff 1995a, 1995b; Ivone Gebara 1989, 1996; Stephen Bede Scharper 1993, 1998), lean heavily upon the Catholic church's long-standing belief in the "preferential option for the poor." It is then a short step to connect human poverty with the profiteering that lies behind so many of our environmental problems. Liberation theology signals the problematic status of wealth for Christians. While having money is not a sin per se, this chapter's title suggests that, for Christians, what wealth might do to a person spiritually ought to be a source of some concern.

> Liberation theology and ecological discourse have something in common; they stem from two wounds that are bleeding. The first, the wound of poverty and wretchedness, tears the social fabric of millions and millions of poor people the world over. The second, systematic aggression against the earth, destroys the equilibrium of the planet, threatened . . . by a type of development undertaken

by contemporary societies, now spread throughout the world. . . . It is time to try and bring the two disciplines together. (Boff 1995a)

Liberation theologians preach the need for political activism to combat the unholy duo of poverty and environmental destruction.

This thumbnail sketch of the four streams of theological scholarship that speak to contemporary environmental crises (Process Theology, New Cosmology, Ecofeminism, and Liberation Theology) ought to be supplemented by reading Stephen Bede Scharper's 1998 book, *Redeeming the Time: A Political Theology of the Environment*, which is (in my opinion) the best book in this area. However, Christians often find their way to God via routes that don't involve the scholarship of theologians. Consider the next section as an example of a (nontheological) Christian response to the environmental crisis.

The Jesus I Meet in the Gospels

The Jesus I meet in the Gospels in many ways is the spitting image of my father. [That would be a difficult statement for any psychologist to make without explanation or apology—but there it is.] I would now like to tell you why I believe that He wants us to walk gently through his creation.

There are two things about Jesus that have emerged from my reading and reflection upon the Gospels. First, his focus was spiritual, and so his battles, values, pain, and contradictions were typically not obvious to casual observers. Thus, the authors of the Gospels focus upon Jesus' words—as they are hints to his inner, spiritual struggles. Occasionally, his actions were so powerful that they were forcefully recounted. For example, going postal on the moneychangers in the temple, or publicly befriending sinners who were so low on the social hierarchy that publicly showing them kindness was enough to scandalize those for whom appearances mattered, were but two examples. Somehow, Jesus suggested, we must learn to look beneath the surface—to see what is in people's hearts. People's interior worlds are often quite different from their external appearances. Jesus was careful to recommend holy harlots (Mary Magdaline) and whitened sepulchers (various Pharisees) for our consideration to alert us to the frequent outer appearance/inner reality dichotomy. Unlike Jesus, we cannot see directly into others' hearts—thus it is necessary for us to examine others' words and deeds very carefully.

The second thing that strikes me about Jesus is that He seemed to genuinely like people. The Gospels tell us that crowds frequently followed him, and his words and deeds often depicted his genuine affection for most people (hypocrites, moneychangers, etc., being the noteworthy exceptions). In these two domains (i.e., seeing what is in people's hearts and genuinely liking most people), my father was as close to Jesus as any human I have known. And while Jesus followed the "will of the Father" in all things, my father knew and followed "nature's ways," rather than the tenets of any organized religion.

True, Jesus led a low ecological impact lifestyle, but we must be careful to not overinterpret that fact. His culture (which developed in a desert region) forced all to make minimal demands on their environment. However, Jesus was quite aware of greed, gluttony, and the waste of God's gifts. He clearly was opposed to these excesses (not because his society experienced overstressed waste sinks, but rather) because they were impediments to normal, spiritual development. Jesus seemed to me to be an environmentalist for spiritual rather than environmental reasons. Thus, the desire for spiritual growth that one finds in every religion might represent an important force in moving people away from our present-day environmental "sins" of overconsumption.

All Judeo-Christian religions seem to have strong profamily traditions. That belief seems completely consistent with my reading of the Gospels. However, some Christian religions (e.g., Roman Catholicism) have extended their beliefs to be pro–large families. While one might develop a preference for large families based upon the 2,000-year history of the church (another source of revelation), I see no evidence suggesting that *large* families represent "a good," in my reading of the Gospels. Quite the contrary. Mary and Joseph had one child; Jesus, himself, had none. Recall that members of the holy family did *not* have large families, even though they lived in a society with a very high birth rate. Similarly, while at least some of the apostles apparently had families before becoming followers of Christ, we find no evidence that they continued to father children subsequently. Quite the contrary, becoming a follower of Christ meant "leaving their family and following Jesus." [As a methodological point, one could argue that these gospel "facts" should be used to bolster the argument for a celibate clergy, and have nothing to do with family size. Perhaps, but I see them as more clearly speaking to family size than to celebacy.] However, interpretation of any text is problematic, and my claim is *not* that these "gospel facts" prove that smaller families are preferred in the Gospels. Rather, I think one needs to stretch mightily to conclude that, on balance, the Gospels furnish support for larger rather than smaller families.

In Which Direction Do the Winds of Change Blow?

Jesus was a remarkably compassionate human being. He seemed to have responded to human suffering whenever He was able—regardless of whether the suffering was produced by disease, guilt, confusion, poverty, personal tragedies, or other causes. Here is a man who truly cared about the well-being of his neighbors. In doing so, He showed us how we can strive to become a bit more God-like.

The data on global overpopulation (reviewed in the introduction) and the record of human and environmental tragedies produced by overpopulation convince me that overpopulation will become the leading cause of human suffering for the twenty-first century. One of the few humane, effective means that we have for combating such mass human suffering is the use of artificial means of birth control. The Jesus that I meet in the Gospels would not have aligned himself against these methods of preempting human suffering. Of course, that represents only my interpretation of his message. I would never promote the use of birth control to anyone whose beliefs suggested he or she should not employ these forms of contraception. Thus, the work on natural birth control should also go forward. From the perspective of world overpopulation, it matters not a whit whether a decline in our growth rate results from the use of natural or artificial means of contraception. And yet, the Catholic Church still finds itself opposed to all artificial forms of birth control.

While one would never wish to have the church base its morality solely upon public opinion, I believe that one of the sources of divine revelation is the beliefs, attitudes, and practices of the people of God. There is ample evidence that Catholic Americans question the church's opposition to birth control. Nine out of ten Catholic Americans do not believe that birth control is wrong. Six out of ten Catholic women of childbearing age are actually using some form of contraception. While these data do not imply that the church must change its position, I believe that these numbers do suggest that the church should once again rethink the wisdom of its opposition to artificial means of birth control in order to ascertain if its position still conforms to the dictates of faith and reason. Given the threats that accompany global overpopulation, and the doubts that many Catholics have about the church's stance against artificial methods of birth control, the time is right to reevaluate the church's stance in light of the current state of the world.

Early Decisions and Tough Choices
Any decision, whether to change or to maintain the status quo on artificial methods of birth control, will be a wrenching one. One cannot change the church's position without worrying about the decision's impact upon a range of issues, from its impact on Catholics' extramarital sexual behavior to the views of the faithful on the church's moral authority. A reevaluation, fol-

lowed by a decision *not* to change the church's position, will undoubtedly produce a negative reaction on the part of many. One thing is clear: The path of least resistance is to avoid the issue.

Maintaining the status quo on birth control, however, poses problems for other Catholic values. For example, many thinkers have maintained that opposition to birth control actually serves to *increase* the incidence of abortion. A similar connection is also made in the environmental science literature, when the effects of cuts in funding of family planning programs are traced. "One reason the world is now facing such dramatic per capita resource declines," writes Lester R. Brown, "is the policy of benign neglect that seems to have affected family planning programs both at the national level and within the international development community. After two decades of strong U.S. leadership in international family planning efforts, the Reagan Administration withdrew all U.S. funding from the United Nations Population Fund and the International Planned Parenthood Federation, the two principal sources of international family planning assistance. Yielding to pressures from the political far right, which used opposition to abortion to cut off this financing, the Administration effectively forfeited leadership. Ironically, as a result more and more Third World women are denied access to family planning services and forced to resort to abortion" (Brown 2001). [While President Clinton reversed Reagan's initiative, George W. Bush's first act as president was to revert to Reagan's bias against family planning both domestically and abroad.]

While the contention that limiting access to birth control results in more abortions is scientifically supported, I am aware of no data that "proves" that relationship exists. But the reader should be wary of overemphasizing the importance of this last sentence. Recall that there still is no proof beyond doubt that cigarette smoking produces lung cancer. However, this fact speaks more to the enormous difficulties involved in proving anything beyond doubt in science than it speaks to the likely causal role of smoking in the genesis of lung cancer.

AIDS represents another problem for the Catholic position on birth control, since, for many sexually active individuals, condom use now represents the only reasonable means of protecting oneself against AIDS. It is a terrible position for anyone to be forced either to violate a moral teaching of his or her religion or to expose oneself to a potentially fatal disease. This quandary is usually (although not always) complicated by the church's position on other issues such as extramarital sex and homosexuality. From a global overpopulation perspective, these other issues (extramarital sex, homosexuality, etc.) pale in significance beside the issue of using artificial means of birth control. It is unfortunate, therefore, if the interaction of these other issues make it more difficult for the church to see the wisdom in reversing its position on artificial means of birth control.

Nothing Endures But Change

A philosopher of science, Stephen Toulmin, claims that the heart of scientific rationality lies not in the finding of timeless truths, but rather in the way in which science changes and improves its beliefs. "A man demonstrates his rationality," he writes, "not by a commitment to fixed ideas, stereotyped procedures, or immutable concepts, but by the manner in which and the occasions on which he changes those ideas, procedures, and concepts" (Toulmin 1961). Having spent a life in the service of science, I recognize the importance of periodic reexaminations of cherished beliefs and subsequent change as vital activities in the progress of science. I find Pope John Paul II's recent willingness to re-evaluate the church's position on the Galileo affair a hopeful sign. It suggests that the church might be more interested in eventually "getting things right" than it is in appearing always to have been right. The heart of the Catholic message lies in a few timeless truths—like love of neighbor—that can easily be extracted from the life of Jesus and his church. However, the church speaks on many topics in ways that are appropriate only in a certain context. I believe we court disaster if we erroneously believe that we must defend such positions as if they represented timeless truths. That the church continues to make such revisions in its beliefs is to me, a promising sign.

In my reading of the Gospels, I find no compelling evidence that Jesus opposed artificial methods of birth control—let alone that this would constitute a timeless truth of his message. Further, while I can well believe that the church's opposition to artificial means of birth control faithfully reflected Jesus' message at some points in history, I find our opposition inappropriate right now. I simply cannot believe that the Jesus I meet in the Gospels would not want to play an active role in preventing the human suffering and environmental degradation that loom before us as a result of global overpopulation. I honestly believe that He wants us to reverse ourselves on this truth that was appropriate for another time.

Conclusion

This chapter offered several approaches to theological thinking (e.g., the new cosmologists, ecofeminist theology, liberationist theology of the environment) that see the current environmental crisis as another source of revelation in our never-ending task of getting the "good news" of Christian revelation right for our times. Christians' distrust of wealth and their antipathy for wasteful, overly consumptive lifestyles make them natural conservationists. Further, Christians' characteristic love of neighbor makes them natural promoters of the common good.

It falls to all Christians to rethink the body of revelation given to us (via scriptures, the history of the people of God, the history of the cosmos, and one's personal experience of good and evil) to obtain a fresh set of Christian truths appropriate for the twenty-first century. The Catholic Church's opposition to most forms of birth control sets it at odds with the environmental movement. The latter part of this chapter represented the author's effort to make the Catholic good news more appropriate for contemporary challenges. I believe that one demonstrates her or his faith in a religious tradition, not by blind obedience to its every belief, but by a loving critique of its weakest tenets with an eye toward improving those beliefs. Or as we say at Notre Dame, "It is not a virtue to accept everything that sources of authority offer on blind faith. God gave you a neocortex. Presumably, He wanted you to use it!"

CHAPTER TWELVE

~

Buddhist Economics

This was by far the most difficult chapter to begin to write. I am an amateur economist—and even more a neophyte in Buddhism. Then why would someone so unqualified even consider writing a chapter on this topic? The answer is simple, my intuition tells me there is something lurking in Buddhism that is profoundly important for this book.

This insight first dawned on me when I read a brief, remarkable chapter entitled "Buddhist Economics" in the book *Small Is Beautiful: Economics as if People Mattered* (Schumacher 1973). But before we consider Shumacher's essay, we must first be introduced to Buddhism. Marvin Levine has a charming way of introducing Buddhism to his readers. He tells the story of Siddhartha—a historical figure, like Jesus and Mohammed, around whom a religion arose: (from M. Levine's *The Positive Psychology of Buddhism and Yoga*).

About 2,600 years ago, the ruler of a small Indian state fathered a son whom he named Siddhartha Gautama. At his birth, it was prophesied that Prince Siddhartha would grow up to be either a great king or a great spiritual leader. Siddhartha's father was clear about his own desires: He wanted his son to be a great king. To this end, the king had his son brought up with definite restrictions. Siddhartha was to be trained in the warrior and governing arts. He was not to receive religious teachings or to know the hardships of life. The father even feared the effects upon Siddhartha of the poverty and misery that might be seen in the surrounding towns. Therefore, he restricted him to the palace grounds. Until he grew to adulthood, Siddhartha did not regard this as confinement, for the grounds extended for miles and included beautiful parks and streams. The most pleasurable entertainments and the friendship of noble children were all his, and he held the status as the king's heir. He thus flourished within these golden walls. When Siddhartha was a young man, his father attached him further to the royal life by having him marry a beautiful princess. Not long after, they had a son.

Siddhartha, now in his 20s, was fully aware of the confined life he had been living. He had simply obeyed his father and had stayed within the palace grounds. Nevertheless, he finally persuaded his father that he, the prince, should view the lands and people that he would one day rule. The king agreed and set a date for Siddhartha's excursion to the nearby villages.

The king, however, took no chances. He sent word to the surrounding communities about the upcoming visit. He ordered that a festive welcome was to be given to his son, that on that day none but the young and healthy were to be seen in their finest, most colorful dress. The old, the sick, and the dying were to be hidden away.

For all his precautions, however, the king failed. The selected day arrives. The prince leaves the palace in a chariot, escorted by Channa, his charioteer. The people, vigorous and colorfully arrayed, line the streets. Shiddhartha is dazzled by the beauty and admiration of the crowd. Suddenly, however, there appears a half-naked man, covered with oozing sores, emaciated from illness, collapsed on the ground. Siddhartha stops the chariot and inquires of Channa what that might be. Is that a human being? Channa replies that he is indeed a human, but that he is ill. Siddhartha asks what it means to be so ill. Is this some sort of punishment? Channa replies that it is not. What has happened to him could happen to any of us. "Even to me?" "Even to you, oh prince."

They ride on through the youthful, cheering throng when a second momentous event occurs. There appears an ancient, decrepit man, wrinkled, eyes clouded over, hanging weakly onto a staff. Again, Siddhartha inquires and again is informed that this is indeed a human and that his condition will be the condition of all of us who live for so many years.

A third event occurs soon after. In the midst of the festivities, a funeral procession appears. Siddhartha, startled by the grey motionless corpse, is informed by Channa that this is death, that the life of every one of us will end in this way.

Siddhartha, troubled, decides to return to the palace. On the way back they pass a man simply dressed, carrying a bowl for begging. He is a forest hermit, a type of spiritual seeker common in India at that time. Nevertheless, he is a novel and puzzling apparition to Siddhartha. Channa explains that the man is one who has withdrawn from the world in order to better understand himself and the world. He follows a path of the spirit.

They reenter the palace, but these four events have transformed Siddhartha. He sees now the potential horrors lurking behind the glittering surface of palace life. He sees his own vulnerability to life's sorrows and the pain that must be in the world. Remembering the fourth event, he decides after a few weeks to become one of these. One night, taking tender leave of his sleeping wife and child, and without telling his father, he leaves the palace. Returning to where he had seen the monk he gives away his expensive clothes, and enters the forest hoping to find kindred souls who might teach him.

Before continuing with the tale, let us note the symbolic significance of Siddhartha's transformation. One might think that renunciation of the world is appropriate only for people who have little and are wretched to start with. Siddhartha, by his action, tells us that is not so. Even princely pleasures cannot compensate for the pain caused by ignorance of life. If we lack understanding, the richest, most luxurious life is not good enough.

We also can make here a comparison between West and East. Psychotherapy in the West is concerned with specific types of suffering: depression, phobias, obsessions, and the like. Buddhism begins with the more general framework of suffering: that derived from illness, aging, and the constant threat of death. As will be seen when we consider the teachings of the mature Buddha, the concept of suffering will be enlarged to cover not only the general framework but the Western clinician's concerns as well as other kinds of pain.

In the forest, Siddhartha meets fellow-seekers. He also finds teachers with whom he studies but who leave him ultimately unsatisfied. He and five other seekers like himself go off together and decide to practice a radical asceticism, literally starving themselves.

One day, when he is alone, Siddhartha faints from hunger. He is found by a young woman who revives and feeds him. Siddhartha realizes that asceticism was not leading him to the answers that he seeks. If anything, by so weakening him, it became a hindrance. As he had earlier rejected the life of pleasure, he now rejects the ascetic life. He understands that he is looking for something between the two, what he will later call The Middle Way.

With this in mind, he enters upon a great meditation. He emerges from it transformed. Not only has he seen the heart of life, but he has formulated his insights as a doctrine. By this vision, this enlightenment, he realizes that he is now beyond the reach of life's horrors, and is suffused by a profound serenity. This transformation is seen even in his outward behavior, with the result that people, sensing his wisdom and serenity, soon start calling him the Buddha, which means the Enlightened (or Awakened) One.

As the Buddha, he returns to his five colleagues in the forest and begins his teaching. They, struck by his remarkable contentment and by the depth of his insights, give up asceticism and become his first disciples. Soon other teachers, leaders of large sects, are won over. They and many of their followers swell the ranks of this new movement. By the time the Buddha is about 40 years old, the movement, although relatively small, is firmly established in India.

The Buddha lived another 40 years, the revered leader of this new "religion." I put the word in quotes because, as will be seen, no assumptions, visions, or beliefs about deity are invoked. In fact, Buddhism today is sometimes referred to as the atheistic religion. (Levine 2000, 9–12)

With that brief historical grounding in Buddhism, you are now prepared for Schumacher's remarkable treatise on Buddhist economics—economics as if people mattered. In contrast, our Western approach to economics worships at the totem of a different God—the unholy trinity of maximization of marginal utilities, maximization of return on investments, and maximization of profits. Three ideas in one very strange God (from E. F. Schumacher's *Small Is Beautiful*):

"Right Livelihood" is one of the requirements of the Buddha's Noble Eightfold Path. It is clear, therefore, that there must be such a thing as Buddhist economics. . . .

Economists themselves, like most specialists, normally suffer from a kind of metaphysical blindness, assuming that theirs is a science of absolute and invariable truths, without any presuppositions. Some go as far as to claim that economic laws are as free from "metaphysics" or "values" as the law of gravitation. We need not, however, get involved in arguments of methodology. Instead, let us take some fundamentals and see what they look like when viewed by a modern economist and a Buddhist economist.

There is universal agreement that a fundamental source of wealth is human labour. Now, the modern economist has been brought up to consider "labour" or work as little more than a necessary evil. From the point of view of the employer, it is in any case simply an item of cost, to be reduced to a minimum if it cannot be eliminated altogether, say, by automation. From the point of view of the workman, it is a "disutility"; to work is to make a sacrifice of one's leisure and comfort, and wages are a kind of compensation for the sacrifice. Hence the ideal from the point of view of the employer is to have output without employees, and the ideal from the point of view of the employee is to have income without employment.

The consequences of these attitudes both in theory and in practice are, of course, extremely far-reaching. If the ideal with regard to work is to get rid of it, every method that "reduces the work load" is a good thing. The most potent method, short of automation, is the so-called "division of labour" and the classical example is the pin factory eulogised in Adam Smith's *Wealth of Nations*.

Here it is not a matter of ordinary specialisation, which mankind has practised from time immemorial, but of dividing up every complete process of production into minute parts, so that the final product can be produced at great speed without anyone having had to contribute more than a totally insignificant and, in most cases, unskilled movement of his limbs.

The Buddhist point of view takes the function of work to be at least threefold: to give a man a chance to utilise and develop his faculties; to enable him to overcome his egocentredness by joining with other people in a common task; and to bring forth the goods and services needed for a becoming existence. Again, the consequences that flow from this view are endless. To organise work in such a manner that it becomes meaningless, boring, stultifying, or nerveracking for the worker would be little short of criminal; it would indicate a greater concern with goods than with people, an evil lack of compassion and a soul-destroying degree of attachment to the most primitive side of this worldly existence. Equally, to strive for leisure as an alternative to work would be considered a complete misunderstanding of one of the basic truths of human existence, namely that work and leisure are complementary parts of the same living process and cannot be separated without destroying the joy of work and the bliss of leisure.

From the Buddhist point of view, there are therefore two types of mechanisation which must be clearly distinguished: one that enhances a man's skill and power and one that turns the work of man over to a mechanical slave, leaving man in a position of having to serve the slave. How to tell the one from the other? "The craftsman himself," says Ananda Oomaraswamy, a man equally competent to talk about the modern west as the ancient east, "can always, if allowed to, draw the delicate distinction between the machine and the tool. The carpet loom is a tool, a contrivance for holding them by the craftsmen's fingers; but the power loom is a machine, and its significance as a destroyer of culture lies in the fact that it does the essentially human part of the work." It is very clear, therefore, that Buddhist economics must be very different from the economics of modern materialism, since the Buddhist sees the essence of civilisation not in a multiplication of wants but in the purification of human character. Character, at the same time, is formed primarily by a man's work. And work, properly conducted in conditions of human dignity and freedom, blesses those who do it and equally their products. The Indian philosopher and economist J. C. Kumarappa sums the matter up as follows:

"If the nature of the work is properly appreciated and applied, it will stand in the same relation to the higher faculties as food is to the physical body. It nourishes and enlivens the higher man and urges him to produce the best he is capable of. It directs his free will along the proper course and disciplines the animal in him into progressive channels. It furnishes an excellent background for man to display his scale of values and develop his personality."

If a man has no chance of obtaining work he is in a desperate position, not simply because he lacks an income but because he lacks this nourishing and enlivening factor of disciplined work which nothing can replace. A modern economist may engage in highly sophisticated calculations on whether full employment "pays" or whether it might be more "economic" to run an economy at less than full employment so as to ensure a greater mobility of labour, a better stability of wages, and so forth. His fundamental criterion of success is simply the total quantity of goods produced during a given period of time. "If the marginal urgency of goods is low," says Professor Galbraith in *The Affluent Society*, "then so is the urgency of employing the last man or the last million men in the labour force." And again: "If . . . we can afford some unemployment in the interest of stability—a proposition, incidentally, of impeccably conservative antecedents—then we can afford to give those who are unemployed the goods that enable them to sustain their accustomed standard of living."

From a Buddhist point of view, this is standing the truth on its head by considering goods as more important than people and consumption as more important than creative activity. It means shifting the emphasis from the worker to the product of work, that is, from the human to the subhuman, a surrender to the forces of evil. The very start of Buddhist economic planning would be a planning for full employment, and the primary purpose of this would in fact be employment for everyone who needs an "outside" job: it would not be the maximisation of employment nor the maximisation of production. Women, on the whole, do not need an "outside" job, and the large-scale employment of women in offices or factories would be considered a sign of serious economic failure. In particular, to let mothers of young children work in factories while the children run wild would be as uneconomic in the eyes of a Buddhist economist as the employment of a skilled worker as a soldier in the eyes of a modern economist.

While the materialist is mainly interested in goods, the Buddhist is mainly interested in liberation. But Buddhism is "The Middle Way" and therefore in no way antagonistic to physical well-being. It is not wealth that stands in the way of liberation but the attachment to wealth; not the enjoyment of pleasurable things but the craving for them. The keynote of Buddhist economics, therefore, is simplicity and non-violence. From an economist's point of view, the marvel of the Buddhist way of life is the utter rationality of its pattern—amazingly small means leading to extraordinarily satisfactory results.

For the modern economist this is very difficult to understand. He is used to measuring the "standard of living" by the amount of annual consumption, assuming all the time that a man who consumes more is "better off" than a man who consumes less. A Buddhist economist would consider this approach excessively irrational: since consumption is merely a means to human well-being, the aim should be to obtain the maximum of well-being with the minimum of consumption. Thus, if the purpose of clothing is a certain amount of temperature comfort and an attractive appearance, the task is to attain this purpose with the smallest possible effort, that is, with the smallest annual destruction of cloth and with the help of designs that involve the smallest possible input of toil. The less toil there is, the more time and strength is left for artistic creativity. It would be highly uneconomic, for instance, to go in for complicated tailoring, like the modern west, when a much more beautiful effect can be achieved by the skilful draping of uncut material. It would be the height of folly to make material so that it should wear out quickly and the height of barbarity to make anything ugly, shabby or mean. What has just been said about clothing applies equally to all other human requirements. The ownership and the consumption of goods is a means to an end, and Buddhist economics is the systematic study of how to attain given ends with the minimum means.

Modern economics, on the other hand, considers consumption to be the sole end and purpose of all economic activity, taking the factors of production—land, labour, and capital—as the means. The former, in short, tries to maximise human satisfaction by the optimal pattern of consumption, while the latter tries to maximise consumption by the optimal pattern of productive effort. It is easy to see that the effort needed to sustain a way of life which seeks to attain the optimal pattern of consumption is likely to be much smaller than the effort needed to sustain a drive for maximum consumption. We need not be surprised, therefore, that the pressure and strain of living is very much less in, say, Burma than it is in the United States, in spite of the fact that the amount of labour-saving machinery used in the former country is only a minute fraction of the amount used in the latter.

Simplicity and non-violence are obviously closely related. The optimal pattern of consumption, producing a high degree of human satisfaction by means of a relatively low rate of consumption, allows people to live without great pressure and strain and to fulfil the primary injunction of Buddhist teaching: "Cease to do evil; try to do good." As physical resources are everywhere limited, people satisfying their needs by means of a modest use of resources are obviously less likely to be at each other's throats than people depending upon a high rate of use. Equally, people who live in highly self-sufficient local communities are less likely to get involved in large-scale violence than people whose existence depends on world-wide systems of trade.

From the point of view of Buddhist economics, therefore, production from local resources for local needs is the most rational way of economic life, while dependence on imports from afar and the consequent need to produce for export to unknown and distant peoples is highly uneconomic and justifiable only in exceptional cases and on a small scale. Just as the modern economist would admit that a high rate of consumption of transport services between a man's home and his place of work signifies a misfortune and not a high standard of life, so the Buddhist economist would hold that to satisfy human wants from faraway sources rather than from sources nearby signifies failure rather than success. The former tends to take statistics showing an increase in the number of ton/miles per head of the population as economic progress, while to the latter—the Buddhist economist—the same statistics would indicate a highly undesirable deterioration in the *pattern* of consumption.

Another striking difference between modern economics and Buddhist economics arises over the use of natural resources. Bertrand de Jouvenel, the eminent French political philosopher, has characterised "western man" in words which may be taken as a fair description of the modern economist:

"He tends to count nothing as an expenditure, other than human effort; he does not seem to mind how much mineral matter he wastes and, far worse, how much living matter he destroys. He does not seem to realise at all that human life is a dependent part of an ecosystem of many different forms of life. As the world is ruled from towns where men are cut off from any form of life other than human, the feeling of belonging to an ecosystem is not revived. This results in a harsh and improvident treatment of things upon which we ultimately depend, such as water and trees."

The teaching of the Buddha, on the other hand, enjoins a reverent and nonviolent attitude not only to all sentient beings but also, with great emphasis, to trees. Every follower of the Buddha ought to plant a tree every few years and look after it until it is safely established, and the Buddhist economist can demonstrate without difficulty that the universal observation of this rule would result in a high rate of genuine economic development independent of any foreign aid. Much of the economic decay of south-east Asia (as of many other parts of the world) is undoubtedly due to a heedless and shameful neglect of trees.

Modern economics does not distinguish between renewable and non-renewable materials, as its very method is to equalise and quantify everything by means of a money price. Thus, taking various alternative fuels, like coal, oil, wood, or water-power: the only difference between them recognised by modern economics is relative cost per equivalent unit. The cheapest is automatically the one to be preferred, as to do otherwise would be irrational and "uneconomic". From a Buddhist point of view, of course, this will not do; the essential difference between non-renewable fuels like coal and oil on the one hand and renewable fuels like wood and water-power on the other cannot be simply overlooked. Non-renewable goods must be used only if they are indispensable, and then only with the greatest care and the most meticulous concern for conservation. To use them heedlessly or extravagantly is an act of violence, and while complete non-violence may not be attainable on this earth, there is nontheless an ineluctable duty on man to aim at the ideal of non-violence in all he does.

Just as a modern European economist would not consider it a great economic achievement if all European art treasures were sold to America at attractive prices, so the Buddhist economist would insist that a population basing its economic life on non-renewable fuels is living parasitically, on capital instead of income. Such a way of life could have no permanence and could therefore be justified only as a purely temporary expedient. As the world's resources of non-renewable fuels—coal, oil and natural gas—are exceedingly unevenly distributed over the globe and undoubtedly limited in quantity, it is clear that their exploitation at an ever-increasing rate is an act of violence against nature which must almost inevitably lead to violence between men.

This fact alone might give food for thought even to those people in Buddhist countries who care nothing for the religious and spiritual values of their heritage and ardently desire to embrace the materialism of modern economics at the fastest possible speed. Before they dismiss Buddhist economics as nothing better than a nostalgic dream, they might wish to consider whether the path of economic development outlined by modern economics is likely to lead them to places where they really want to be. . . .

It is in the light of both immediate experience and long-term prospects that the study of Buddhist economics could be recommended even to those who believe that economic growth is more important than any spiritual or religious values. For it is not a question of choosing between "modern growth" and "traditional stagnation." It is a question of finding the right path of development, the Middle Way between materialist heedlesness and traditionalist immobility, in short, of finding "Right Livelihood." (Schumacher 1973, 50–58)

Conclusions

If you are enjoying this chapter, then you really ought to read more of Levine's (2000) and Schumacher's (1973) books. The former fleshes out the psychology that lies behind Buddhism and Yoga (two paths that lead to a mature happiness), while the latter paints a portrait of an economics that values people (and our planet) over the maximization of various other things (like profits, consumables, etc.). Both books are important (in a general way) because they offer one a profoundly different way of seeing our world. For example, I read the business section of the New York Times almost every day. In these pages, it is almost always assumed that the trinity of maximized goods (noted above) is the supreme (and often the only) value to be honored. I always blink after reading a Times business article, and ask myself, "How would a Buddhist economist see that situation?"

Similarly, being a psychologist, I often speak with troubled people. After trying to understand their difficulties via diagnostic categories, personality dynamics, stressful life events, and the like, I often think of Levine asking, "What cravings (Tanka) make this person vulnerable to suffering (Dukkha)? Which practices of the eightfold path (Magga) might produce liberation

(Nirvana)?" Levine's is an important vision for psychology—one that they never taught me in graduate school.

Finally, many potential applications of Buddhist thought extend far beyond the topics considered in this book. For example, I believe youth sports programs today are often being ruined because of coaches', players', and parents' fanatical preoccupation with winning. In *Coaching Matters: Youth Sports as Preparation for Life* (Howard 2002) I suggest three alternative goals that coaches might entertain *instead* of focusing on winning:

> Exactly what do parents want their children to get from youth sports? From the Buddhist perspective, the goal of any life experience is to help children learn "right livelihood"—or how to live in accord with the flow of the Universe (i.e., the Tao). E. F. Schumacher (in *Small Is Beautiful*) translates this nebulous concept (right livelihood) into three concrete goals appropriate for youth sports:
>
> (1) to give a young person a chance to utilize and develop her or his skills;
>
> (2) to enable him or her to overcome their natural egocenteredness by joining with other kids in a common task; and
>
> (3) to create exciting entertainment for his or her team, the opposition, and spectators.
>
> Notice that we do *not* have winning as one of our goals. Further, since domination is the antithesis of right livelihood, a blowout should be a source of profound embarrassment to the coach of the *winning* team. It would be like a skilled dancer moving in a way that highlights her or his dancing partner's ineptness. Real skill in dancing means one's partner appears to be a better dancer than he or she typically is. To coax the very best out of both our team and our opponent in a close, exciting contest represents the ultimate coaching skill. (Howard 2002)

Do those three alternative goals sound familiar to you? They ought to. You just read the source of inspiration for my three goals. [Go back and reread the fifth paragraph in Schumacher's essay that begins "The Buddhist point of view. . . ."] In fact, Phil Jackson (*Sacred Hoops: Confessions of a Hardwood Warrior*) claims that a Buddhist approach to basketball yields an unintended, positive consequence—winning! Right (basketball) livelihood leads to winning—even thought it is not a primary goal per se. Jackson's eight (and counting) NBA Championships suggest he might know what he's talking about, when the topic is winning. One can easily see that Buddhist thought speaks to many disparate aspects of our lives.

Like most readers, I am a novice in this chapter's topics. Thus, I have only been able to point toward the paths that lead toward a Buddhist psychology and a Buddhist economics. However, a Buddhist philosophy of life can serve as a powerful antidote to many of the excesses in Western ways of thinking that have produced the environmental problems our world now faces. For example, the first section of this book dramatized how maximization and perfectionism often imply people inflicting their will upon the course of events in their lives. The Western approach is to *want certain things* to happen in my life" (e.g., success, happiness, a loving family) and then to work hard to make these desired outcomes come about. That Western, instrumental orientation is a mistake, from a Buddhist perspective. Rather, one should *want what will happen"* in life. The Tao cannot be changed—our task is to become comfortable with (i.e., to genuinely want) what will happen (i.e., what the Tao has in store for us). Thus, we are to participate in the flow of nature (i.e., to swim with the current of life) rather than attempting to change the flow of life. As we'll see more clearly in the next chapter on Gandhi's seven sins, the Eastern way is to use simple, noninvasive, moderate means to achieve Nirvana in our lives.

⁓

CHAPTER THIRTEEN

Gandhi's Seven Sins

Mohandas K. Gandhi is a Hindu political and spiritual leader who was instrumental in India's struggle for independence from British rule. The easiest way to acquaint yourself with the *political* struggles of Gandhi is through producer/director Richard Attenborough's (1982) award-winning film, *Gandhi*. By reviewing his political campaigns in South Africa and India, the movie demonstrates why Gandhi is acknowledged as a leading political figure of the twentieth century. However, the movie barely alludes to the *spiritual* career of the Mahatma (meaning "great soul"). It is the spiritual journey of Gandhi that makes him a worthy subject for any book on how we should lead our lives in the twenty-first century.

Gandhi (1948/1983) wrote an unusual autobiography entitled *Gandhi's Autobiography: The Story of My Experiments with Truth*. This work reveals (in a realistic, human way) the life and struggles of the Mahatma, which are both glorified and oversimplified in the movie *Gandhi*. Rather than being a God-like figure who was so much better and wiser than his contemporaries, the autobiography allows Gandhi to show his life as a long, painful series of experiments that inexorably led him to *his truth*—which in his mind was synonymous with God. It was Gandhi's series of personal, spiritual experiments with life (e.g., practicing nonviolence in his relationships, celibacy in marriage, implementing dietary restrictions) that bear relevance for the topics of this book. His political actions, and his cultivation of the principle of *satyagraha* (or nonviolence) that the movie portrays, represent significant achievements. However, it is the personal philosophy that evolved out of Gandhi's experiments with truth that is most important for our question,"How should we live our lives?"

While Gandhi was familiar with the sacred scriptures of many religions (e.g., the Buddhist *Bhagavad Gita*, the Muslim *Koran*, the Judeo-Christian *Old and New Testaments*) he saw them as (perhaps) co-equal sources of nuggets of religious wisdom that served to knit together the results of his experiments with truth (from his life experiences). This fusion of diverse sacred texts with personal experiments led him inexorably to his understanding of God. In the earlier chapter on Christian thought, we saw a believer's personal experiences in life as one (among four) sources of divine revelation. Gandhi elevated the results of his personal experiments with truth into principle virtues for which he took vows (*satyagraha* [nonviolence], nonpossession, *brahmacharya* [celibacy], body labor, control of the palate, and others). What for Gandhi began as experiments in various disciplines of restraint and self-purification ended as personal vows that he adhered to with fanatical zeal (and at times near-catastrophic consequences) for himself and members of his family.

The portrait of Gandhi that emerges from his autobiography is that of an extraordinarily earnest seeker of truth (and of God) who saw his life-experiences as critical experiments in his dogged search for answers as to how he should live his life. Most of us will *not* arrive at the same lifestyle as the Mahatma (who practiced celebacy in his own marriage; would not drink milk because of how cows were treated; and would not wear machine-spun cloth because it deprived workers of hand-spun cloth of their right livelihood). Rather, we should admire Gandhi's willingness to see beyond society's taken-for-granted beliefs about how one should think and act. Gandhi's uniqueness lies in his willingness to apply higher values to his own actions, and to accept the consequences of holding oneself to these higher, spiritual standards. Perhaps more than anyone, Gandhi realized that his life and actions were not his private property—he knew that his behaviors would profoundly impact many others. Rather than shying away from that enormous responsibility, he welcomed the opportunity to demonstrate a lifestyle that if practiced by all others would optimize the common good.

Extremism and Balance in Life

In many ways, Gandhi was an unyielding extremist—a fanatic of the first order. His autobiography humbly recounts several instances where his extreme beliefs got him and his loved ones into grave difficulties. One senses that these faux pas were included to demonstrate that following one's beliefs often leads one astray in the short run. However, one needs to accept such missteps in order to find God in the long run, as failures represent an integral (and inevitable) part of the total process of searching earnestly for truth. However, Gandhi realized that in honestly struggling toward a good, one could inadvertently do mischief.

The autobiography also reveals Gandhi to be a person who knew what was right and what was wrong in spiritual matters. He was unbending in his beliefs. While he was willing to discuss his views with others who disagreed with him, his views never seemed to be changed by the arguments. This unwillingness to change or compromise extended to areas that were less clearly "spiritual issues," such as his determination to join an ambulance corps in World War I, his insistence that his wife not be given beef broth (for medicinal purposes) when she was seriously ill, and the like. In sum, Gandhi was a complex, driven, and uncompromising visionary who was an extremist in every sense of the word. Paradoxically, his form of extremism led to spiritual beliefs and associated lifestyles that might serve as models for the twenty-first century. His was a very responsible extremism.

Gandhi's extremism was responsible because of his acute sense of the need for balance in human lives. The seven sins that are inscribed on the Mahatma's tomb in Delhi show his appreciation for the need for balance in all human affairs. For example, in the Judeo-Christian Ten Commandments, actions are identified as either good (e.g., keep holy the Sabbath) or evil (e.g., killing, stealing), and we are ordered to do what is good and avoid what is evil. Sin, then, is defined as instances where one does evil or fails to do good. Gandhi believed in this straightforward notion of virtue and sin, and he lived his life accordingly.

However, Gandhi also offered seven sins (or the things that will destroy us) that are far more complex in form than the simple "do this" and "don't do that" approach noted above. From this second perspective, avoiding sin also requires that we *balance* two "goods" simultaneously. Pursuing one "good" without the balance offered by the pursuit of a complimentary "good," represents a sin to Gandhi. The seven sins are:

> *Wealth without work*
> *Pleasure without conscience*
> *Knowledge without character*
> *Commerce without morality*
> *Science without humanity*
> *Religion without sacrifice*
> *Politics without principle*

Let's consider the sin "Wealth without work" first. As you know from the previous chapter, the main function of work is not to achieve wealth. Work, from a Buddhist perspective, is an important part of right livelihood. If one makes work decisions primarily with an eye toward maximizing wealth, rather than with an eye toward achieving enlightenment, then one courts sin. Gandhi knows that work also provides most people with the ability to purchase the basics in life. However, Gandhi also sees that few people are able to separate their career and work choices from monetary considerations, even after their basic needs have been more than met. Instead of making work an important means to enlightenment, the lust for maximum profits and wealth leads people (and companies also) to make choices that lead to serious exploitation of others.

Gandhi himself led the nonviolent battle against English mill cloth because tending huge machines (usually by performing a robotic task as part of an assembly line) would not provide right livelihood for members of the British working class. However, even more important, the British mills deprived enormous numbers of Asian Indians the *spiritual* benefits (not to mention a way to scrape out a modest living) of engaging in the craft of making homespun cloth. The solution for Indians was to *prefer* the coarser (lower quality) and more expensive (because it is not mass-produced by machines) homespun cloth to the output of the British mills. Gandhi felt this "economically stupid" purchasing decision should be made because the spiritual benefits of a homespun cloth production system are preferred to mere economic considerations. The subtitle of E. F. Schumacher's *Small Is Beautiful* is *Economics as if People Mattered*. Gandhi takes that sentiment one step further; he urges all to make work decisions based upon spiritual considerations rather than economic (in a Western maximizing sense) imperatives.

The *voluntary simplicity* movement teaches us to see value in simple pleasures and simple means to beneficial ends. Downsizing our lives opens our attention to pleasures of the interior life (e.g., spirituality, family, community sharing, the fine arts) as we gradually free ourselves from the grip of external shackles such as materialism, the headlong pursuit of wealth, consumerism, political power, fame, and the like. Gandhi might serve as a beacon in our search to recapture the older spiritual values that American culture has ignored because of its twentieth-century fascination with power and growth.

One could profitably meditate upon each of Gandhi's seven sins, as they apply to the environmental challenges that loom before us. A few general observations about the structure of all seven of his sins follows.

Acts of Balance

The opposite of extremism is moderation. It is easy to understand why it is important to balance polar opposites. Politically, wild-eyed liberals and doctrinaire conservatives are both impediments to good political processes. This is because of the intransigence of both extreme groups—recall the maxim that "Politics is the art of compromise." Too often, extremists are unwilling to compromise even when middle of the road (or compromise) solutions are called for.

However, Gandhi's seven sins pose a more thorny intellectual problem than the balancing of opposites. How could "Religion," for example, be bad (or dangerous) unless it is accompanied by "Sacrifice?" Why is "Science without Humanity" problematic?

Covey (1998) describes the sin in "Religion without Sacrifice" in the following manner:

> Without sacrifice we may become active in a church but remain inactive in its gospel. In other words, we go for the social façade of religion and the piety of religious practices. There is no real walking with people or going the second mile or trying to deal with our social problems that may eventually undo our economic system. It takes sacrifice to serve the needs of other people—the sacrifice of our own pride and prejudice, among other things.
>
> If a church or religion is seen as just another hierarchical system, its members won't have a sense of service or inner worship. Instead they will be into outward observances and all the visible accoutrements of religion. But they are neither God-centered nor principle-centered. (91)

So there you have it! Myopically fixating on anything—even if it is a good thing (e.g., religion, science, wealth)—is dangerous and ultimately can become sinful.

Once again, simple-minded extremism is suspect wherever it rears its ugly head because it lacks the balance that characterizes enlightened thought. Gandhi showed us how to wrestle with many issues simultaneously. Further, he urged us to undertake small experiments each day that test ourselves with respect to various spiritual issues (e.g., nonviolence, celibacy, vegetarianism, etc.). Out of the resulting melange of partial insights, context-dependent rules of thumb, and experience-tested beliefs will slowly emerge a balanced understanding of the terrible complexity of life. One will slowly come to know his or her truth. And the Great Soul called his evolving understanding of good and evil in the world—God.

CHAPTER FOURTEEN

~

Conclusion: Changing
Human Societies

Perhaps it would be helpful to recap this book's thesis, which was laid out in the introduction. Our looming environmental problems suggest that something is profoundly wrong with human societies as we pass from the twentieth to the twenty-first century. A multitude of scientific studies concur as to the roots of our maladies—too many people leading unsustainable lifestyles. Our planet simply can not support this level of human activity—we are behaving in a nonsustainable manner. I concur with the overwhelming majority of thinkers (e.g., Ehrlich and Ehrlich 1991; Gore 1992; Hardin 1993; Hawken 1993; Scharper 1998) who see our present problems as springing from various psychological, spiritual, economic, and political roots. The bulk of this book probed some interconnections among the various causes of our present set of environmental problems. Indeed humans, and the societal structures they created, are the causes of our present environmental problems. And what are the prospects for reversing our troubling environmental trends?

This book focuses readers on their present attitudes. We must examine our attitudes toward money, perfectionism, success, green taxes, voluntary simplicity, conspicuous consumption, individualism, community, our spiritual values, and a host of other dimensions. Thus, I believe that changing humans' attitudes represents an important first step in solving our environmental problems. However, there is an extensive research literature in psychology (Black, Stern, and Elworth 1985; Guagnano, Stern, and Dietz

1995; Gardner and Stern 1996; McKenzie-Mohr 2000) that shows that proenvironmental attitudes (and changes in those attitudes) are only weakly related to more proenvironmental behaviors, especially in the presence of strong proconsumption environmental factors (e.g., low gas prices). Is this not a problem for my thesis?

Gradually environmentalists have come to realize that our economic and business systems are more powerful determinants of our pro- or antienvironmental behaviors than we had imagined. It takes an uncommonly dedicated person to live a life of voluntary simplicity when she or he is trapped within grossly wasteful economic and business systems. It is clear that the American systems that now nurture our unsustainable lifestyles must change before individuals' proenvironmental wishes can be transformed into sustainable, earth-friendly lifestyles. But how does one influence change in societal structures?

One way to promote change is by exerting political pressure to change the structure. Allow me to give one current example. President George W. Bush came to office amid the California energy crisis of 2000–2001. A special task force (chaired by Vice President Dick Cheney) analyzed the problem and concluded that "conservation won't solve the problem" and that the country was going to drill its way out of this mess (i.e., produce and burn more oil, natural gas, and coal). The public's reaction to this antienvironmental proposal was more negative than positive, and the Democratic opposition in Congress became more vocal in their support of proenvironmental, alternative energy proposals (e.g., solar, wind, geothermal) as well as the technologies of cleanliness and efficiency, (e.g., clean-burning gas-to-liquid fuels, fuel cells, hydrogen storage). The critical political question then became "How would the average American (those nonextremists on the question of carbon-based versus alternative energy economic structures) react?" Notice that it will be the attitudes of moderate Americans toward the issues analyzed in this book that will rule the day.

Almost immediately, the Bush administration beefed up the tax benefits for alternative energy in their energy plan. Perhaps the administration sensed that the typical American was skeptical about a completely carbon-based, increase-production solution. The administration's energy proposal inched a bit closer to the political center.

However, about the same time, the administration had to decide whether the United States would sign the Kyoto accord on reducing greenhouse gases. The administration made its decision, and the *New York Times* sadly reported, "178 nations reach a climate accord; U.S. looks on." Remarkably, a few days later the following article appeared in the *Seattle Times*, "Despite White House reluctance, Seattle to adopt Kyoto limits." The citizens of the state of Washington had fired a shot over the Bush administration's bow. Apparently the typical Washington citizen is more favorably disposed toward the Kyoto accord than is the Bush administration. But perhaps the administration already knew that their "drill-bit energy plan" and the rebuff of the Kyoto accord would put them too far out of step with the ever-more environmentally concerned "typical American." For as they were rejecting Kyoto, the administration was strongly endorsing the hydrogen economy—the clean and renewable energy system of the future. Thus, our story returns to some of our old friends (from chapter 9)—Stan Ovshinsky and Energy Conversion Devices, with their "from sunshine to a Sunday drive" complete solution to our energy and pollution problems (at least from burning carbon-based fuels).

On July 18, 2001, Texaco (with a bevy of congressmen present) announced that they and ECD were embarking upon a joint venture to manufacture Ovonic Nickel Metal Hydride Batteries in large volumes to meet the anticipated explosion in electric, hybrid electric, and fuel cell automobiles. When an old-line oil company like Texaco invests about $500 million (20 percent of ECD's stock and investments in batteries, hydrogen storage, and fuel cell joint ventures) in a small hydrogen economy company, then even big business seems to be sending a message to our political leaders as to what our energy future holds. Texaco (indeed all business) must read the attitudes of consumers (people like you); just as politicians must read the attitudes of voters (people like you also). Your environmental attitudes are crucial in changing the business and political institutions that now force us to live unsustainable lifestyles.

If someone wanted to write a cynical summary of this book, it might sound something like this,

> *How Should I Live My Life?* is an extended exercise in propaganda! Howard's view is that the best future for the earth lies in the clean, renewable, and efficient technologies of the hydrogen economy, as opposed to our present carbon-based system. He tries to show that his vision of the future is preferable on psychological, economic, political, and moral grounds. He also thinks we should dramatically curtail the human population—preferably through a birth rate solution. He is trying to get readers to think more like him because doing so would slowly change the business, economic, political, and religious systems that have shaped our present unsustainable lifestyles.

While a little less than charitable, that cynical summary is not untrue. So you see it comes down to our choices—as citizens of our country, as consumers, as investors, and as believers. William James had some wisdom about making choices when the options are complex and uncertain, and the stakes are enormous.

> We stand on a mountain pass in the midst of whirling snow and blinding mist, through which we get glimpses now and then of paths which may be deceptive. If we stand still we shall be frozen to death. If we take the wrong road we shall be dashed to pieces. We do not certainly know whether there is any right path. What must we do? Be strong and of a good courage. Act for the best, hope for the best, and take what comes. . . . If death ends all, we cannot meet death better. (James 1896/1956, 30–31)

Less than a decade ago, a different presidential administration floated the idea of a carbon tax (a green tax on all carbon-based energy sources). The idea failed to fly politically and all we got for our effort was a small, temporary gas tax—not even passed on environmental grounds, but as a way to rein in our enormous federal budget deficits. We (both individually and as a political body) chose a decade ago to continue the carbon-based energy policies of the past. And what have been the consequences of this choice? I'll leave that to each reader to answer.

The proposed carbon tax was unsuccessful. However, we are once again setting our nation's energy future. Will we be more successful this time around? It is too early to tell as I write this conclusion. Good luck to each of us, as we make the many choices that will collectively determine how we will live the rest of our lives.

Postscript

The ultimate extremist acts occurred on September 11, 2001. Both towers of the World Trade Center were destroyed by crashing hijacked commercial airliners into the buildings. Once again, extremism leads to disaster.

This event also causes me to marvel at the prescience of Father Hesburgh's list of the five most important educational topics for the twenty-first century.

1. peace
2. justice
3. human rights
4. an ecumenical view of religion
5. environmental problems

References

Albee, G. W. 1977. "The Protestant Ethic, Sex, and Psychotherapy." *American Psychologist* 32: 150–61.

Attenborough, R. 1982. *Gandhi*. Hollywood, Calif.: Columbia Studios.

Bartholomew, R. E., and Howard, G. S. 1998. *UFOs and Alien Contact: Two Centuries of Mystery*. Amherst, N.Y.: Prometheus.

Bateson, G. 1979. *Mind and Nature: A Necessary Unity*. New York: Dutton.

Bellah, R. N., Madsen, R., Sullivan, W. M., Swindler, A., and Pipton, S. M. 1985. *Habits of the Heart: Individualism and Commitment in American Life*. New York: Harper and Row.

Berzins, J. I. 1977. "Therapist-Patient Matching." In A. S. Gurman and A. M. Razin, eds., *Effective Psychotherapy: A Handbook of Research*. New York: Pergamon.

Bettelheim, B. 1976. *The Uses of Enchantment: The Meaning and Importance of Fairy Tales*. New York: Knopf.

Beutler, L. E. 1981. "Convergence in Counseling and Psychotherapy: A Current Look." *Clinical Psychology Review* 1: 79–101.

Beutler, L. E., Clarkin, J., Crego, M., and Bergan, J. 1990. "Client-Therapist Matching." In C. R. Snyder and D. R. Forsyth, eds., *Handbook of Social and Clinical Psychology*. New York: Pergamon.

Black, J. S., Stern, P. C., and Elworth, J. T. 1985. "Personal and Contextual Influences on Household Energy Adaptations." *Journal of Applied Psychology* 70: 3–21.

Boff, L. 1995a. *Ecology and Liberation: A New Paradigm*. Translated by John Cumming. Maryknoll, N.Y.: Orbis Books.

———. 1995b. "Liberation Theology and Ecology: Alternative, Confrontation or Complementary?" In L. Boff and V. Elizondo, eds., *Ecology and Poverty: Cry of the Earth, Cry of the Poor*. Vol. 5 of *Concilium*. Maryknoll, N.Y.: Orbis Books.

Boulding, K. E. 1966. "The Economics of the Coming Spaceship Earth." In H. Jarrett, ed., *Environmental Quality in a Growing Economy*. Baltimore, Md.: Johns Hopkins University Press.

Brislin, R. W. 1988. *Increasing Awareness of Class, Ethnicity, Culture, and Race by Expanding on Students' Own Experiences*. The G. Stanley Hall Lecture Series, no. 8. Washington, D.C.: APA.

Brown, J. M. 1989. *Gandhi: Prisoner of Hope*. New Haven, Conn.: Yale University Press.

Brown, L. R. 2001. *Eco-economy: Building an Economy for the Earth*. New York: Norton.

Bruner, J. 1986. *Actual Minds, Possible Worlds*. Cambridge, Mass.: Harvard University Press.

Campbell, D. T. 1975. "On the Conflicts between Biological and Social Evolution and between Psychology and Moral Tradition." *American Psychologist* 30: 1103–26.

Carkhuff, R. R., and Pierce, R. 1967. "Differential Effects of Therapists' Race and Social Class upon Patient Depth of Self-Exploration in the Initial Clinical Interview." *Journal of Consulting Psychology* 31: 632–34.

Carson, R. 1962. *Silent Spring*. Boston: Houghton-Mifflin.

Cobb, J. B. Jr. 1972. *Is It Too Late? A Theology of Ecology*. Beverly Hills, Calif.: Bruce.

——. 1982. *Process Theology as Political Theology*. Philadelphia: Westminster.

Collins, S. D. 1974. *A Different Heaven and Earth*. Valley Forge, Pa.: Judson Press.

Constantinople, A. P. 1973. "Masculinity-Femininity: An Exception to a Famous Dictum." *Psychological Bulletin* 80: 389–407.

Corporation for Public Broadcasting. 1994. *The Diamond Empire*. Frontline, N.Y.: Corporation for Public Broadcasting.

Covey, S. R. 1998. *Principle-Centered Leadership*. London: Simon & Schuster.

Cronbach, L. J. 1982. *Designing Evaluations of Educational and Social Programs*. San Francisco: Jossey-Bass.

Cushing, J. 1994. Review of "Too hot to handle: The Race for Cold Fusion." *Philosophy of Science* 55: 1–4.

Donahue, M. J. 1994. "Reflections on 'Reflections.'" *International Journal of Psychology and Religion* 4: 151–56.

Dougherty, F. E. 1976. "Patient-Therapist Matching for Prediction of Optimal and Minimal Therapeutic Outcome." *Journal of Consulting and Clinical Psychology* 44: 889–97.

Durning, A. 1991. "Asking How Much Is Enough." In L. R. Brown, ed., *The State of the World: 1991*. New York: Norton.

Durning, A. T. 1992. *How Much Is Enough? The Consumer Society and the Future of the Earth*. New York: Norton.

Efran, J. S., Lukens, R. J., and Lukens, M. D. 1988. "Constructivism: What's in It for You?" *The Family Therapy Networker* 12: 27–35.

Ehrlich, P. R. 1968. *The Population Bomb*. New York: Ballantine.

——. 2000. *Human Natures: Genes, Cultures, and the Human Prospect*. Washington, D.C.: Island Press.

Ehrlich, P. R., and Ehrlich, A. H. 1990. *The Population Explosion.* New York: Simon & Schuster.

———. 1991. *Healing the Planet.* Reading, Mass.: Addison Wesley.

Frazer, J. G. 1890. *The Golden Bough: A Study of Magic and Religion.* London: Macmillan.

Fry, P. S., and Charron, P. A. 1980. "Effects of Cognitive Style and Counselor-Client Compatibility on Client Growth." *Journal of Counseling Psychology* 27: 529–38.

Gandhi, M. K. 1983. *Autobiography: The Story of My Experiments with Truth.* New York: Dover.

Garbarino, J. 1995. *Raising Children in a Socially Toxic Environment.* San Francisco: Jossey-Bass.

Gardner, G. T., and Stern, P. C. 1996. *Environmental Problems and Human Behavior.* Needham Heights, Mass.: Allyn and Bacon.

Gardner, H. 1985. *The Mind's New Science: The History of the Cognitive Revolution.* New York: Basic Books.

Gebara, I. 1989. *Mary, Mother of God, Mother of the Poor.* Maryknoll, N.Y.: Orbis Books.

———. 1996. "The Trinity and Human Experience." In R. R. Reuther, ed., *Women Healing Earth: Third World Women on Ecology, Feminism, and Religion.* Maryknoll, N.Y.: Orbis Books.

Geertz, C. 1973. *Interpretation of Cultures.* New York: Basic Books.

Gergen, K. J. 1989. Personal letter dated December 13, 1989.

Glendinning, C. 1995. "Technology, Trauma, and the Wild." In T. Roszak, M. Gomes, and A. Kanner, eds., *Ecopsychology: Restoring the Earth, Healing the Mind.* San Francisco: Sierra Club Books.

Gore, A. 1992. *Earth in the Balance: Ecology and the Human Spirit.* New York: Penguin.

Guagnano, G., Stern, P. C., and Dietz, T. 1995. "Influences on Attitude-Behavior Relationships: A Natural Experiment with Curbside Recycling." *Environment and Behavior* 27: 699–718.

Hall, D. J. 1986. *Imaging God: Dominion as Stewardship.* Grand Rapids, Mich.: Eerdmans.

———. 1990. *The Steward: A Biblical Symbol Come of Age.* Grand Rapids, Mich.: Eerdmans.

Hardin, G. 1968. "The Tragedy of the Commons." *Science* 162: 1243–48.

———. 1993. *Living Within Limits: Ecology, Economics, and Population Taboos.* New York: Oxford University Press.

Hawken, P. 1993. *The Ecology of Commerce.* New York: HarperCollins.

Hawking, S. W. 1988. *A Brief History of Time: From the Big Bang to Black Holes.* New York: Bantam.

Henderson, H. 1981. *The Politics of the Solar Alternatives to the Economics Age.* Garden City, N.Y.: Anchor/Doubleday.

Herrnstein, R. J. 1990. "Rational Choice Theory: Necessary But Not Sufficient." *American Psychologist* 45: 356–67.

Hillman, J. 1975. *Re-visioning Psychology.* New York: Harper and Row.

Holdren, J. 1990. "Energy in Transition." *Scientific American* 263: 156–63.

————. 1991. "Population and the Energy Problem." *Population and Environment* 12: 231–55.

Howard, G. S. 1985. "The Role of Values in the Science of Psychology." *American Psychologist* 40: 255–65.

————. 1986. "Food Can't Keep Pace with Population." *Chicago Tribune*, 13 April 1986, p. 20.

————. 1989. *A Tale of Two Stories: Excursions into a Narrative Approach to Psychology*. Notre Dame, Ind.: Academic Publications.

————. 1991. "Culture Tales: A Narrative Approach to Thinking, Cross Cultural Psychology, and Psychotherapy." *American Psychologist* 46: 187–97.

————. 1992. "No Middle Voice." *Journal of Theoretical and Philosophical Psychology* 12: 12–26.

————. 1993. *Understanding Human Nature: An Owner's Manual*. Notre Dame, Ind.: Academic Publications.

————. 1994a. "Reflections on Change in Science and Religion." *International Journal of Psychology and Religion* 4: 127–43.

————. 1994b. "Some Varieties of Free Will Worth Practicing. *Journal of Theoretical and Philosophical Psychology* 14: 50–61.

————. 1997. *Ecological Psychology: Creating a More Earth-Friendly Human Nature*. Notre Dame, Ind.: University of Notre Dame Press.

————. 2002. *Coaching Matters: Youth Sports as Preparation for Life*. University of Notre Dame.

Howard, G. S., and Conway, C. G. 1986. "Can There Be an Empirical Science of Volitional Action? *American Psychologist* 41: 1241–51.

Howard, G. S., Delgado, E., Miller, D., and Gubbins, S. 1993. "Transforming Values into Actions: Ecological Preservation through Energy Conservation." *The Counseling Psychologist* 21: 581–95.

Jackson, P. 1995. *Sacred Hoops: Spiritual Lessons of a Hardwood Warrior*. New York: Hyperion.

James, W. 1890. *The Principles of Psychology*. New York: Holt.

————. 1896. *The Will to Believe*. New York: Scribner.

Kagitcibasi, C., and Berry, J. W. 1989. "Cross-Cultural Psychology: Current Research and Trends." In M. R. Rosenzwig and L. W. Porter, eds., *Annual Review of Psychology*, vol. 40. Palo Alto, Calif.: Annual Reviews.

Keller, C. 1986. *From a Broken Web: Separation, Sexism, and Self*. Boston: Beacon.

————. 1996. *Apocalypse Now and Then: A Feminist Guide to the End of the World*. Boston: Beacon Press.

Landfield, A. W. 1971. *Personal Construct Systems in Psychotherapy*. Chicago: Rand McNally.

Lave, L., Russell, A. G., Hendrickson, C. T., and McMichael, F. C. 1996. "Battery-Powered Vehicles: Ozone Reduction versus Lead Discharges." *Environmental Science and Technology* 30: 401–7.

Leavitt, D. 1986. *The Lost Language of Cranes*. New York: Knopf.

Leopold, A. 1949. *A Sand County Almanac*. New York: Oxford University Press.

Levine, M. 2000. *The Positive Psychology of Buddhism and Yoga.* Englewood Cliffs, N.J.: Earlbaum Associates.

LeVine, R. A. 1984. "Properties of Culture: An Ethnographic View." In R. Shweder and R. LeVine, eds. *Culture Theory: Essays in Mind, Theory, and Emotion.* Cambridge: Cambridge University Press.

Levy-Bruhl, L. 1910. *Les functions mentales dons les societes inferieures.* Paris: Alcan.

Lyddon, W. J. 1989. "Personal Epistemology and Preference for Counseling." *Journal of Counseling Psychology* 36: 423–29.

Mair, M. 1988. "Psychology as Storytelling." *International Journal of Personal Construct Psychology* 1: 125–38.

———. 1989. *Between Psychology and Psychotherapy.* London: Routledge.

Malthus, T. 1798. "An Essay on the Principle of Population." In G. Hardin, ed. 1964. *Population, Evolution, and Birth Control: A Collage of Controversial Readings.* San Francisco: Freedman.

Mander, J. 1991. *In the Absence of the Sacred.* San Francisco: Sierra Club Books.

Maritain, J. 1931. *Religion and Culture.* Translated by J. F. Scanlan. London: Sheed and Ward.

Markus, H. and Nurius, P. 1986. "Possible Selves." *American Psychologist* 41: 954–69.

McAdams, D. 1985. *Power, Intimacy, and the Life Story.* Homewood, Ill.: Dorsey Press.

———. 1993. *The Stories We Live By: Personal Myths and the Making of the Self.* New York: Morrow.

McDaniel, J. B. 1989. *Of God and Pelicans: A Theology of Reverence for Life.* Philadelphia: Westminster.

———. 1990. *Earth, Sky, Gods, Mortals: Developing an Ecological Spirituality.* Mystic, Conn.: Twenty-Third Publications.

McFague, S. 1987. *Models of God: Theology for an Ecological, Nuclear Age.* Philadelphia: Fortress.

———. 1993. *The Body of God: An Ecological Theology.* Minneapolis: Fortress.

McKenzie-Mohr, D. 2000. "Fostering Sustainable Behavior through Community-Based Social Marketing." *American Psychologist* 55: 531–37.

Meadows, D. H., Meadows, D. L., and Randers, J. 1992. *Beyond the Limits.* White River Junction, Vt.: Chelsea Green.

Merrill Lynch. 1997. Advertisement brochure. New York.

Miller, G. A., Galanter, E., and Pribrim, K. H. 1960. *Plans and Structure of Behavior.* New York: Holt.

Ming-Dao, D. 1983. *The Wandering Taoist.* San Francisco: Harper and Row.

New York Times. "178 Nations Reach a Climate Accord; U.S. Only Looks On," 24 July 2001, p. 1.

Nisbett, R., and Ross, L. 1980. *Human Inference: Strategies and Shortcomings of Social Judgment.* Englewood Cliffs, N.J.: Prentice Hall.

Noethe, J. 2000. "Bridging the Gap: An Empirically-Supported Phenomenological Study of Environmental Living." Ph.D. diss., University of Notre Dame.

Ornstein, R., and Ehrlich, P. 1989. *New World / New Mind.* New York: Doubleday.

Oskamp, S. 2000. "Psychology for a Sustainable Society." *American Psychologist* 55: 496–508.

Passell, P. August 29, 1996. "Another Accepted Truth Under Fire: Electric Cars = Cleaner Air." *New York Times*, 2(D).

Plomin, R. 1990. *Nature and Nurture: An Introduction to Human Behavioral Genetics.* Pacific Grove, Calif.: Brooks/Cole.

Polkinghorne, D. P. 1988. *Narrative Knowing and the Human Sciences.* Albany, N.Y.: SUNY Press.

Redford, R. 1994. *Quiz Show.* Hollywood, Calif.: Hollywood Home Pictures.

Reuther, R. R. 1975. *New Woman / New Earth: Sexist Ideologies and Human Liberation.* New York: Seabury.

———. 1983. *Sexism and God-Talk: Toward a Feminist Theology.* Boston: Beacon.

Robbins, L. G. 1989. *Uncommon Cents: Benjamin Franklin's Secrets to Achieving Personal Financial Success.* Salt Lake City, Utah: Franklin International Institute.

Rychlak, J. F. 1989. *The Psychology of Rigorous Humanism.* 2d ed. New York: New York University Press.

Sahlins, M. 1976. *Culture and Practical Reason.* Chicago: University of Chicago Press.

Sarbin, T. R., ed. 1986. *Narrative Psychology: The Storied Nature of Human Conduct.* New York: Praeger.

Schank, R. C., and Abelson, R. P. 1977. *Scripts, Plans, Goals, and Understanding.* Hillsdale, N.J.: Erlbaum.

Scharper, S. B. 1998. *Redeeming the Time.* New York: Continuum.

Scharper, S. B., and Cunningham, H. 1993. *The Green Bible.* Maryknoll, N.Y.: Orbis Books.

Seattle Times, July 25, 2001. "Despite White House Reluctance, Seattle to Adopt Kyoto Limits," p. 1.

Schmidheiny, S. 1992. *Changing Course: A Global Business Perspective on Development and the Environment.* Cambridge, Mass.: MIT Press.

Schneider, D. M. 1968. *American Kinship: A Cultural Account.* Englewood Cliffs, N.J.: Prentice Hall.

Schumacher, E. F. 1973. *Small Is Beautiful.* New York: Harper and Row.

Schwartz, B. 1986. *The Battle for Human Nature: Science, Morality, and Modern Life.* New York: Norton.

Shiva, V. 1989. *Staying Alive: Women, Ecology, and Development.* London: Zed Books.

———. 1991. *The Violence of the Green Revolution: Third World Agriculture, Ecology, and Politics.* London: Zed Books.

Shweder, R. A. 1984. "Anthropology's Romantic Rebellion against the Enlightenment, or There's More to Thinking than Reason and Evidence. In R. A. Shweder and R. LeVine, eds., *Culture Theory.* Cambridge: Cambridge University Press.

Simon, H. A., and Newell, A. 1964. "Information Processing in Computer and Man." *American Scientist* 53: 281–300.

Sober, E., and Wilson, D. S. 1998. *Unto Others: The Evolution and Psychology of Unselfish Behavior.* Cambridge, Mass.: Harvard University Press.

Spence, D. P. 1982. *Narrative Truth and Historical Truth: Meaning and Interpretation in Psychoanalysis*. New York: Norton.

Stein, M. L., and Stone, G. L. 1978. "Effects of Conceptual Level and Structure on Initial Interview Behavior." *Journal of Counseling Psychology* 25: 96–102.

Sue, S. 1988. "Psychotherapeutic Services for Ethnic Minorities." *American Psychologist* 43: 301–8.

Tanney, M. F., and Birk, J. M. 1976. "Women Counselors for Women Clients?: A Review of the Research." *The Counseling Psychologist* 6: 28–31.

Toulmin, S. E. 1961. *Foresight and Understanding: An Enquiry into the Aims of Science*. Bloomington: Indiana University Press.

Triandis, H. C. 1972. *The Analysis of Subjective Culture*. New York: Wiley.

Turiel, E. 1979. "Distinct Conceptual and Developmental Domains: Social Convention and Morality." In C. B. Keasy, ed., *Nebraska Symposium on Motivation*, vol. 25. Lincoln: University of Nebraska Press.

Turner, V. 1967. *The Forest of Symbols*. Ithaca, N.Y.: Cornell University Press.

Tyler, E. B. 1871. *Primitive Culture*. London: Murray.

United Nations. 1998. *Energy Statistics Yearbook*. New York: United Nations Publications.

U.S. Department of Commerce. 1996. *World Population Profile*. Washington, D.C.

Varian, H. 2000. "What Will Happen If We Tax Gasoline Like Europeans Do?" *New York Times*, 19 October 2000, 2(B).

Will, G. F. 1983. *Statecraft as Soulcraft*. New York: Simon & Schuster.

Wilson, E. O. 1992. *The Diversity of Life*. New York: Norton.

Whorf, B. L. 1956. *Language, Thought, and Reality*. Cambridge, Mass.: MIT Press.

Index

About the Author

George S. Howard is professor of psychology at the University of Notre Dame. A researcher in applied psychology and research methods, he has written numerous books and articles including *Basic Research Methods in the Social Sciences* and *Ecological Psychology: Creating a More Earth-Friendly Human Nature*. Howard is a faculty fellow in the Kroc Institute for International Peace Studies, the Reilly Center for Science, Technology, and Values, and the Erasmus Institute at the University of Notre Dame. He also serves as the Morahan Director of the College of Arts and Letters' Core Course.